HEBREWS

HEBREWS

◆

H. A. IRONSIDE

Revised Edition

Introductory Notes by
John Phillips

LOIZEAUX
Neptune, New Jersey

Hebrews
First Edition © 1932
by the American Bible Conference Association,
Philadelphia.

Combined Edition (with James and Peter) 1982
Revised Edition © 1996 by Loizeaux Brothers

A Publication of Loizeaux Brothers, Inc.
*A Nonprofit Organization Devoted to the Lord's Work
and to the Spread of His Truth*

Unless otherwise indicated, Scripture quotations are from
the King James version of the Bible

Verses marked (RSV) are taken from
the Revised Standard version

Profile taken from *Exploring the Scriptures*
© 1965, 1970, 1989 by John Phillips

Library of Congress Cataloging-in-Publication Data

Ironside, H. A. (Henry Allan), 1876-1951.
Hebrews / H. A. Ironside.—Rev. ed.
Originally published: Philadelphia:
American Bible Conference Association, 1932
ISBN 0-87213-412-1 (alk. paper)
1. Bible. N. T. Hebrews—Commentaries. I. Title.
BS2775.3.I76 1997
227'.8707—dc20   96-9604

Printed in the United States of America
10 9 8 7 6 5 4 3 2 1

CONTENTS

A PROFILE

HEBREWS
OUTSIDE THE CAMP

BY JOHN PHILLIPS

There is considerable divergence of opinion concerning the author of the book of Hebrews. Luke, Barnabas, Clement of Rome, Apollos, and the apostle Paul have all been suggested. The arguments for a Pauline authorship are weighty enough despite the objections made. It is claimed that Paul could not have been the author of Hebrews because the language, the style, and the arguments are not Pauline. Moreover, the Epistle is anonymous whereas Paul's other Epistles all bear his signature. Against this it can be argued that whatever differences in style and language Hebrews may contain as compared with the known Pauline Epistles, the thoughts and the reasonings are very much like Paul's. In addition, all of Paul's other Epistles were addressed to Gentiles whereas Hebrews was written for Jews. But it should not be forgotten that Paul could describe himself as "a Hebrew of the Hebrews" (Philippians 3:5). The suspicion with which the Jews regarded Paul and their deep hatred of him would in itself be ample reason for his withholding his name from any general epistle addressed to them. The closing verses of the Epistle could well have come from Paul (13:18-19). And the reference made to "my bonds" (10:34) and to Timothy (13:23), and the characteristically Pauline "Grace be with you all" (13:25), suggest that the Epistle may not be so anonymous as is sometimes claimed.

One reason why no human name is appended to Hebrews meets us in the first verse, for this is the only Epistle that begins with the

7

divine name in its opening sentence. How authoritative and commanding and important this letter must be. And how right and proper it is that all human authors should sink from sight before that name above all names.

The Epistle to the Hebrews and the Epistle to the Romans have certain similarities profitable to bear in mind. Romans heads the list of the Pauline Epistles, and Hebrews heads the list of the general Epistles. Romans expounds and explains the believer's relationship to the moral law, and Hebrews expounds and explains the believer's relationship to the ceremonial law. Romans moves from law to grace, and Hebrews, from shadow to substance.

Hebrews can be analyzed according to the theme of superiority: the superior person of Christ, the superior provisions of Calvary, and the superior principles of Christianity.

I.   THE SUPERIOR PERSON OF CHRIST (1:1–2:18)
    A. Superior in His Majesty as Son of God (1:1–2:4)
       1. How This Is Expressed (1:1-3)
       2. How This Is Exemplified (1:4-14)
          a. His Excellent Name (1:4-5)
          b. His Earthly Frame (1:6-7)
          c. His Eternal Claim (1:8-14)
       3. How This Is Experienced (2:1-4)
          a. By Appropriating the Gospel (2:1-3a)
          b. By Appreciating the Gospel (2:3b-4)
    B. Superior in His Ministry as Son of Man (2:5-18)
       1. His Sovereignty as Man (2:5-9a)
       2. His Sufferings as Man (2:9b-10)
       3. His Sympathy as Man (2:11-18)
II. THE SUPERIOR PROVISIONS OF CALVARY (3:1–10:39)
    A. We Have a Better Savior (3:1–8:5)
       1. His Pre-eminence (3:1–4:13)
          a. Two People Considered (3:1-6)
          b. Twin Perils Considered (3:7–4:3)
             (1) God's People in the Wilderness in Old Testament Times (3:7-19)

          (2) God's People in the World in New
                Testament Times (4:1-3)
      c. True Peace Considered (4:4-13)
          (1) Creation Rest (4:4-5)
          (2) Canaan Rest (4:6-8)
          (3) Calvary Rest (4:9-13)
    2. His Priesthood (4:14–8:5)
      a. He Is a Rightful Priest (5:4–6:20)
          (1) The Choice of Christ as Priest (5:4-10)
          (2) The Challenge of Christ as Priest
                (5:11–6:20)
                (a) To Those Who Are Weak (5:11–6:3)
                (b) To Those Who Are Wicked (6:4-8)
                (c) To Those Who Are Wise (6:9-20)
      b. He Is a Royal Priest (7:1–8:5)
          (1) His Lordship as Priest (7:1-10)
          (2) His Legality as Priest (7:11-22)
          (3) His Life as Priest (7:23–8:5)
B. We Have a Better Security (8:6-13)
    1. Based on an Improved Covenant (8:6)
    2. Based on an Imperative Covenant (8:7-8)
    3. Based on an Important Covenant (8:9-12)
    4. Based on an Implemented Covenant (8:13)
C. We Have a Better Sanctuary (9:1-12)
    1. The Human Tabernacle (9:1-10)
    2. The Heavenly Tabernacle (9:11-12)
D. We Have a Better Sacrifice (9:13-28)
    1. What Was Wrought by Christ's Sacrifice (9:13-28)
      a. The Old Transgressions Are Removed Forever
          (9:13-14)
      b. The New Testament Is Ratified Forever
          (9:15-28)
          (1) Our Benefits (9:15)
          (2) Our Benefactor (9:16-28)
                (a) His Death Conveys Our Inheritance
                    (9:16-22)

Background of the Epistle

To understand the primary emphasis of Hebrews it should be remembered that it was written to recently converted Jews in the very early days of Christianity. Upon those new Jewish believers the old religious customs of Judaism still exerted a powerful force. The Jewish temple, for example, was still standing, crowning the summit of mount Moriah with magnificent splendor. With all its gorgeous rituals and its elaborate system of sacrifices it beckoned the Jewish convert to Christ to come back to its fold. Jewish traditions, born and bred into the Jewish believer's heart, still powerfully called him to come back to Judaism. The grandest names in history were associated with that religion. Traditions hoary with antiquity pulled upon all the pious emotions, national sentiments, and even religious superstitions of the Jewish believer. The temptation to go back must have been great indeed. Jewish ties of family, friendship, and fellowship were very strong. Those ties had enabled the Jew to overcome persecution and resist assimilation for centuries. Now, by the new believer's conversion to Christ, they were all threatened with severance. During Christ's life on earth the Pharisees had opposed the gospel. And now, during the period covered by the book of Acts, the Sadducees resisted the gospel. Jewish opposition commenced with the persecution of Peter and climaxed in the persecution of Paul. It began in Jerusalem and spread far and wide throughout the dispersion. Moreover, the church was becoming increasingly Gentile in composition, and that was an added problem to the Jewish convert. The Jewish teachings were hard to renounce. Hot and fierce were the debates against Christianity in those early days. How dare the Jewish Christians set aside the law of Moses, the Aaronic priesthood, the solemn rites and rituals of the sacrificial system? So all in all the new convert from Judaism to Christianity had many problems to face, all of which the Epistle to the Hebrews was designed to answer.

Summary of the Epistle

One of the key terms in Hebrews is the word *better* (1:4; 6:9; 7:7; 7:19,22; 8:6; 9:23; 10:34; 11:16,35,40; 12:24). The writer wanted his fellow Jewish believers to see that in Christ they had gained much more than they had renounced in Judaism. Christ was better than the prophets and the angels, superior to Moses and to Joshua, and had a priestly ministry far superior to that of Aaron. The Christian had better promises, a better sanctuary, a better covenant, a better country, and a better resurrection. It was far better to worship in the true heavenly tabernacle than in a man-made temple on earth. The sacrifice of Calvary rendered obsolete all the ceremonial washings and offerings required under the Mosaic law.

The writer of Hebrews repeatedly emphasized the word *heavens* and often employed the adjective *heavenly* (1:10; 3:1; 4:14; 6:4; 7:26; 8:1,5; 9:23,24; 10:34; 11:16; 12:22,23,25,26). His purpose was to show that, in contrast with Judaism, which is earthly and concerned with physical ceremonies, Christianity is heavenly and spiritual. Another vital truth is connected with the word *once*, and the expression, *once for all* (6:4; 7:27; 9:12,26,28; 10:2,10; 12:26,27) intended to convey the truth of the absolute finality of the Christian revelation. It can readily be seen how those truths would encourage Jewish Christians who, for Christ's sake, had gone "[outside] the camp, bearing his reproach" (13:13).

The book of Hebrews is punctuated by five warning passages, and no survey can be complete that does not take them into consideration.

What we must remember is that those warnings are varied in character and scope. They need to be studied in two ways—first in light of their context, to see why they were introduced and where they lead; then in light of their content, to see what they say and to whom they are addressed.

Warning Against Disregarding the Salvation of God (2:1-4)

The warning against disregarding the salvation of God is brief. The writer has just finished setting before us the superior majesty and ministry of Christ. He warns us that we need to pay special heed to what God has to say about His Son. To "neglect so great salvation" as that provided in Christ is a deadly sin. The punishment is spiritual. Those who neglect God's salvation never enter into spiritual life. For them there is no escape.

Warning Against Disbelieving the Sufficiency of God (3:7–4:13)

The context of the passage deals with Israel's sad failure in the Old Testament to enter into rest. God brought a whole generation of Hebrews out of Egypt, but they would not let Him bring them into Canaan. The writer of Hebrews wrote about creation rest and Canaan rest and then of Calvary rest. He warned that it is possible to have a

saved soul but a lost life. The punishment is temporal. The unbelievers in the Old Testament lived a second-class life in the wilderness instead of entering into Canaan rest. It is possible for the Christian, too, to miss the joy, the blessing, the fullness, the fruitfulness,
and the rest that God offers in Christ. In other words—to be saved,
but "so as by fire."

Warning Against Discrediting the Son of God (5:11–6:20)

The context speaks of Christ as our Great High Priest—a real,
rightful, and royal priest, His priesthood based on the superior order of Melchizedek. The warning is threefold. One part is addressed
to those who are weak, one part to those who are wicked, and one
part to those who are wise. At the heart of the warning is a solemn
statement about the impossibility of ever bringing back to the point
of salvation those who, having been fully enlightened, turn away
and thus crucify the Son of God afresh. The punishment is eternal.
The key word is the word *impossible*. It is a terrible word. Other
uses of it in the Epistle underline its finality. "It [is] impossible for
God to lie" (6:18). "It is not possible that the blood of bulls and of
goats should take away sins" (10:4). "Without faith it is impossible
to please [God]" (11:6).

Warning Against Despising the Spirit of God (10:26-39)

The context is solemn. The greatest spiritual privilege was accorded just once a year in Israel to only one man. Once a year, after
elaborate preparation, the high priest could venture inside the veil.
Now all believers can come, as often as they like, for as long as they
like, whenever they like. The writer warns his readers that it is sadly
possible for a person to examine this new covenant and then to turn
back deliberately to a dead religion. In so doing they do despite to
the Spirit of grace. The punishment is judicial. Such apostasy means
that the transgressor will fall into the hands of the living God—
something so fearful that such a possibility should be shunned at all
costs.

Warning Against Disobeying the Summons of God (12:15-29)

The writer had been talking about the heroes of faith. He had been telling of men and women who in the face of all kinds of pressure dared to believe God. He urged the true believer to emulate their example and press on and not to be like Esau, who traded spiritual things for carnal things. Then when he wanted the spiritual too, he found he had lost out forever. The punishment is millennial. The writer continued by drawing a vivid contrast between Sinai and Zion in order to press home his point. It is possible to be in the family of God and yet to be a sad loser in the Kingdom of God.

Such is the book of Hebrews. Truly it is one of the most magnificent books in the Bible. Its teaching is particularly relevant to those coming to Christ out of a dead, Christ-denying religious system.

The Epistle ends with strong emphasis on faith, hope, and love and with an urgent exhortation to live out practically on earth all that is implied in our position in the heavenlies.

INTRODUCTION

W ho wrote Hebrews? Is it for us to be certain in regard to its human author? Is it of any importance that we should know since the letter comes to us anonymously? If God meant us to know the author's name would He not have told us? These are questions properly raised, and I desire to try to answer them in all fairness.

Authorship

I write for those who believe in the inspiration of this Epistle, as of all Scripture. By the term *all Scripture* I mean all that was accepted as Scripture in our Lord's day—that is, the entire Old Testament—as well as the books regarded as canonical by the Christians of the first century. Hebrews belongs to this latter collection and is an integral part of the Word of God. Cut from our Bibles, it would leave a great gap that nothing else could fill. In its place, Hebrews fills that gap admirably and forms in a most marvelous way the connecting link between the economy of the Old and the New Testaments.

The authorship of Hebrews is accredited to Paul the apostle in many of our English Bibles, as also in many manuscripts. Yet from the latter part of the second century many have denied its Pauline authorship. It has been variously ascribed to Apollos, Barnabas, and even to Priscilla, the wife of Aquila! It is strange, if Apollos were the author, that the Alexandrian church never seems to have heard of it, and yet Apollos was of Alexandria. Were he the author, how natural that this church should have had a holy pride in the recognition of his work, and never have permitted his name to be forgotten as the chosen instrument. So far as Barnabas is concerned, there is not a scintilla of evidence that he was its author. The difference in style between other writings ascribed to Barnabas and the Epistle to the Hebrews is too marked to admit of the thought that they could have been written by the same person. As to Priscilla's authorship, in spite of "certain dainty feminine touches" that a lady expositor thinks she has seen in it, the supposition may be rejected as utterly absurd, and without any foundation in fact.

But does it really make any difference as to who the human author was? I think it does, at least in our understanding of its scope and timeliness. This letter is the last of a series of three Epistles forming together a divinely inspired commentary on one Old Testament text, namely Habakkuk 2:4, "The just shall live by his faith." Romans expounds the first two words and shows who alone are "the just" before God. Galatians continues the wondrous story and explains how the just "shall live." Having begun in the Spirit they are not to be made perfect by the flesh, but they live by the same faith that justifies. Hebrews completes the story, showing that it is "by faith" God's pilgrim people walk through this world to His praise and glory. Is it likely that He who is a God of order chose Paul to write Romans and Galatians, but selected some unknown writer to give us Hebrews? Is it not very much more probable that the same servant wrote all three Epistles?

Our second question is, may we be certain as to its human authorship, or is it merely a matter of intellectual speculation at best? I believe God has given us definite information on this point. First, we have the well-known statement of the apostle Peter, which would seem conclusive as to the Pauline authorship:

And account that the longsuffering of our Lord is salvation; even as our beloved brother Paul also according to the wisdom given unto him hath written unto you; As also in all his epistles, speaking in them of these things; in which are some things hard to be understood, which they that are unlearned and unstable wrest, as they do also the other scriptures, unto their own destruction (2 Peter 3:15-16).

It should be noted that the apostle Peter wrote to the Jewish believers scattered abroad, as his first Epistle makes evident. Therefore, of course, he wrote to Hebrews. His second Epistle was written to the same people: "This second epistle, beloved, I now write unto you; in both which I stir up your pure minds by way of remembrance" (2 Peter 3:1). He declared that "our beloved brother Paul" had written an epistle unto them (3:15). Now if Peter was not referring to this letter to the Hebrews, then there is no such letter preserved since Paul's other Epistles were written to companies of saints in Gentile churches.

Then again in this Hebrew letter to which Peter referred, Paul has written "some things hard to be understood, which they that are unlearned and unstable wrest...unto their own destruction" (2 Peter 3:16). How true is this of the Epistle to the Hebrews! How many thousands of unstable souls have been thrown into greatest agony of mind and perturbation of spirit because of misunderstandings and utterly false interpretations of parts of chapters six and ten. It would seem that Peter could not have indicated more definitely than he has done that he referred to this letter to the Hebrews.

Further, in the Epistle to the Thessalonians we read "The salutation of Paul with mine own hand, which is the token in every epistle: so I write. The grace of our Lord Jesus Christ be with you all" (2 Thessalonians 3:17-18). In this verse the apostle Paul wrote of the secret mark, if we may call it that, placed at the end of every one of his letters, thus guarding saints from deception by forgery. Remember the warning in 2 Thessalonians 2:2, "That ye be not soon shaken in mind or be troubled, neither by spirit, nor by word, nor by letter as from us, as that the day of Christ is at hand." What is this secret mark? It is a message that characterized his entire ministry: a salutation that emphasized the grace of our Lord Jesus Christ. Let us notice how this secret mark is found at the close of all his genuine letters.

Romans 16:24: "The grace of our Lord Jesus Christ be with you all. Amen." (Observe verses 25-27 are in the nature of a postscript. The Epistle properly ends with verse 24.)

1 Corinthians 16:23-24: "The grace of our Lord Jesus Christ be with you. My love be with you all in Christ Jesus. Amen."

2 Corinthians 13:14: "The grace of our Lord Jesus Christ, and the love of God, and the communion of the Holy Ghost be with you all. Amen."

Galatians 6:18: "Brethren, the grace of our Lord Jesus Christ be with your spirit. Amen."

Ephesians 6:24: "Grace be with all them that love our Lord Jesus Christ in sincerity. Amen."

Philippians 4:23: "The grace of our Lord Jesus Christ be with you all. Amen."

Colossians 4:18: "The salutation by the hand of me, Paul. Remember my bonds. Grace be with you. Amen."

1 Thessalonians 5:28: "The grace of our Lord Jesus Christ be with you. Amen."

2 Thessalonians 3:18: "The grace of our Lord Jesus Christ be with you all. Amen."

1 Timothy 6:21: "Grace be with thee. Amen."

2 Timothy 4:22: "The Lord Jesus Christ be with thy spirit. Grace be with you. Amen."

Titus 3:15: "All that are with me salute thee. Greet them that love us in the faith. Grace be with you all. Amen."

Philemon 25: "The grace of our Lord Jesus Christ be with your spirit. Amen."

Now look at Hebrews 13:25: "Grace be with you all. Amen." Can there be any question but that here we have Paul's authentication of this letter as written by himself?

The proof becomes stronger when we turn to the general Epistles, and notice how different are all the endings. Never once is the word *grace* used excepting in 2 Peter 3:18. There it is "grow in grace," which is experience, and not the grace that saves. The book of Revelation which is of an altogether different character does use the grace salutation which is quite in keeping with the closing of the New Testament, and we need to remember that it is not an epistle, but a great prophetic treatise.

But why then is the Epistle to the Hebrews given anonymously? I think there is a very clear answer for this. Paul is here writing to his own brethren after the flesh. They were greatly prejudiced against him and his ministry, though he yearned after them with all the fervor of devoted brotherly love. Yet many of them repudiated his apostleship and feared his attitude toward their ancient ritual. He had tried to overcome this opposition. Upon the occasion of his last visit to Jerusalem, he went so far, in accordance with the suggestion of James, as to pay for the sacrificial offerings of certain brethren about to be released from Nazarite vows. But God would not permit this, for it would have been a virtual denial of the sufficiency of the one offering of the Lord Jesus Christ on the cross, and so the divinely permitted insurrection against Paul saved him from this apparent inconsistency (see Acts 21). Probably during the time of his release, after his first imprisonment and before his second arrest (cf. Hebrews 13:23), he was chosen of God to write this letter. In the letter he called on believers in the Lord Jesus to separate completely from Judaism, as the entire system was about to be definitely rejected with the destruction of the Jewish temple so soon to take place. Paul therefore acts in accordance with the principle laid down elsewhere, "Unto the Jews I became as a Jew that I might gain the Jews" (1 Corinthians 9:20). And so he hid his identity and did not insist on his own apostolic authority, but rather made his appeal to the Old Testament Scriptures, in the light of the new revelation.

Scope

Hebrews, then, is the New Testament Leviticus. What Augustine thought of the two Testaments may be very properly limited to these two books. Hebrews is in Leviticus concealed; Leviticus by Hebrews is revealed. This New Testament letter opens up in a marvelous way the typical teaching of the third book of the law. As that book was given to the people of Israel while still in the wilderness, so this is a letter for wilderness saints; for believers who have left this Egypt world behind, and are a pilgrim host journeying on to the rest that awaits the people of God. It is the pilgrim's progress from the cross to the coming glory, and therefore it is a call to separation. These believers are called on to leave:

(a) The shadows for the substance.

(b) The types for the anti-types. (Or rather, the anti-type for the reality, for in this Epistle what we generally call the types are actually designated anti-types, and their fulfillment becomes a reality.)

(c) The good things of Judaism for the better things of Christianity.

(d) The incompleteness of the old dispensation for the perfection of the new.

(e) The carnal ordinances serving a temporary purpose for the eternal spiritual verities of the fuller revelation.

(f) The earthly sanctuary and all its passing ceremonies for the heavenly sanctuary and its abiding realities.

(g) The conditional promises of the old covenant for the unconditional promises of the new. (For although the new covenant has not yet actually been made with Israel and Judah, believers now come under its spiritual blessings.)

In a manner that grips the heart and stirs the mind to its deepest depths, this Epistle points out Christ's glories as Son of God and Son of man. It brings before us in the fullest possible way, His marvelous person as the Apostle and High Priest of our confession. It presents Him as the One who is far superior to angels through whom the law was given; to prophets through whom God gave partial revelations of His mind; to Moses, the apostle of the old dispensation; to Aaron and his successors, the high priests of the earthly sanctuary; and to Joshua who led them into their temporal inheritance. All these are superseded and surpassed by our Lord Jesus Christ. Then His work is shown to be the fulfillment of all the former shadows. This work comes before us as partially executed on earth, and now going on in Heaven. His sacrifice on the cross is absolutely perfect and cancels every other, having settled forever the sin question. His intercession in the heavens above sustains His people through all their wilderness journey, and will be carried on continuously until He comes again.

Although written particularly for the enlightenment of Jewish believers, it is, of course, for all Christians to the end of the dispensation, for in Christ Jesus there is neither Jew nor Greek. What is true for one is now true for all. How sad to undervalue so precious a portion of the Word on the plea that it is "Jewish," and does not give the full Christian position. The fact of the matter is, it was written to deliver Christians from being Jewish, and to bring them into the full light of the glory shining through the torn veil.

In this dispensation of the grace of God, when "in Christ Jesus there is neither Greek nor Jew," it ought to be evident that all the New Testament Epistles are for all the church of God, no matter to whom they may have been first addressed. This does not make it necessary to overlook the fact that there may be in some of them special applications to local conditions now passed away. But all Scripture is for the guidance and instruction of those who belong to Christ and are waiting for His return from Heaven.

Outline of the Epistle

In studying any book of the Bible, it is most important to have a clear outline in mind. In this, as in doctrinal matters, we may well give heed to the apostle's admonition in 2 Timothy 1:13, "Hold fast the form of sound words," or, as it has been otherwise translated, "having an outline of sound words." This will save from many incongruous interpretations and applications. He who selects a text at random from a given book with little or no regard to the context, failing utterly to grasp the theme and its unfolding, is almost certain to be misled and to mislead his ignorant hearers. At the same time he will arouse the pity or contempt of those better instructed.

For our present study I submit the following outline. We have already seen that the theme is the superiority of the New Testament realities to the types and shadows of the former dispensation. In unfolding this theme we find that the Spirit of God apparently divides the Epistle into five parts. These may be displayed as follows:

I. THE GLORIES OF THE SON OF GOD (1:1–2:4)
   A. God Speaking in the Son (1:1-4)

This outline corresponds very closely to that of F. W. Grant in the *Numerical Bible* to which the reader is referred for further help.

According to this outline, the first division (1:1–2:18) emphasizes the great truth that the One in whom God has now spoken is infinitely superior to all the prophets whose writings compose the Old Testament, though it is the same God who speaks in both. But He speaks in fullness in His Son, which was impossible through merely human instruments. The Son is also seen as superior to all angels, for however great their power and might, they are still creatures, but He is the Creator of all things. Throughout this division He is viewed as the Son who has come into the world as man, but who is nevertheless truly God. For it was not until He became incarnate that God could be said to have spoken in Him. He was the Word from all eternity, but the Word was uttered in time when He came into the world as the virgin-born Son of God. It is of all importance to believe and to hold fast the revelation that has been given concerning His glorious Person.

In the second division (2:5–4:13) it is rather the manhood of Christ that is in view. He who is God has become man, and as man He is the prototype of what all men should be and of what all shall yet be who are saved through Him. He became man in order that He might tread the path of faith before us. He entered sinlessly into all human experiences and always sought the glory of the Father. But this alone would not have fitted Him to be the Captain of our salvation. As such, He must be perfected through the suffering of the cross. Ever perfect in Himself as to His character, He nevertheless had to go through the process of perfecting as Savior. In other words, He could not have delivered us from the judgment due to our sins without bearing that judgment Himself. In this division, He is seen to be vastly superior to Moses, the great apostle of the old dispensation, and to Aaron, its high priest. Moreover, it is evident that the house built by Moses, the tabernacle in the wilderness in which Moses himself was but a servant, was designed of God to picture both the universe and the people of God as the habitation of the Spirit, over which the man Christ Jesus, now glorified, is set in authority as Son.

Though now forever beyond the reach of pain and suffering, His tenderness and sympathy are with all His people in the trials they are called to endure. As the Good Shepherd He leads them on through the wilderness to the rest that awaits and will await unbroken through eternity. Even now the trusting soul enters that rest by faith.

In the third division (4:14–10:39), which is by far the longest, we have the very heart of this wonderful Epistle. The heavenly sanctuary is here opened to the eye of faith, and there within the veil our Lord Jesus Christ is seen officiating as our Great High Priest. He is touched with the feeling of our infirmities, ministering to all the needs of His saints on earth, and yet ever representing them perfectly before the throne of God. His priesthood is unchangeable because, properly speaking, it begins on the resurrection side of death. Having died on the cross for our sins, He now lives to die no more, so He will never be superseded by another priest. Nor is His priesthood after the Aaronic or Levitical order. He is both King and Priest at one time after the order of Melchisedec; but be it carefully observed, after the pattern of Aaron. The instruction given in the Old Testament concerning the Aaronic priesthood was all designed to picture Christ's glorious Person and wondrous work.

Having settled the sin question on earth, He has passed through the created heavens into the holiest, the immediate dwelling place

of God, and there has taken His seat as our Forerunner, our Intercessor, and as the Mediator of the new covenant. The veil that separated the holy place from the holiest of all, picturing the flesh of
Christ, was torn at His death. Now the way is open for God to come
out to man and for man to go in to God. In Christ, man has already
entered into the holiest place, for He is the archetypal man, the First-
born among many brethren who will all eventually be conformed to
His blessed image. They have been given the same right to enter in
as He Himself has, namely, His personal perfection and His finished work.

In Hebrews 6 and 10 we are given solemn warnings against the
terrible possibility of apostasy. These warnings were especially for
many from among the Jews who professed faith in Jesus as their
Messiah, but had never really trusted Him as their Savior. Anyone
who has had much experience in dealing with troubled souls knows
that Satan has often used these passages to distract uninstructed yet
sensitive people who have not learned to distinguish between apostasy and backsliding. Some teachers who should know better have
attempted to explain these warnings but have only made more confusion. We will examine these passages in detail in their proper
context. But here it may be well to say that no born again person
will ever become an apostate, for the indwelling Holy Spirit will
guard him from that dreadful state. Backsliding is another thing
altogether, and probably few of us realize how often we are guilty
of it. Any Christian who is not at the present time enjoying Christ as
much as he did in a past day, or living for God as devotedly as he
once did, is just to that extent a backslider.

The word *backslider* is not a New Testament term at all. We find
it only once in the Bible, in Proverbs 14:14. There we read, "The
backslider in heart shall be filled with his own ways." The word
backsliding is found many times, though only in Jeremiah and Hosea.
But while these terms are not found in the New Testament, we have
many warnings against the condition of soul to which they apply,
and it is only too evident that the experience of backsliding is most
common. How great the mercy of God that bears with our manners
in the wilderness and restores our souls when we wander from Him!

When we come to the fourth division (Hebrews 11) what a delight it is to see how God discerns the least evidence of faith working in the souls of His people. What lessons are unfolded in this wonderful honor roll of faith. This chapter is designed by God to spur us on to tread the same path of faith in the power of the Holy Spirit, looking unto Jesus.

The fifth division (Hebrews 12–13) emphasizes the practical ways that should characterize those who have believed the truth revealed in this Epistle. This section also makes clear that the great object in writing this Epislte was to separate those who believed in the Lord Jesus from the temple and the synagogue. Believers are led outside the camp of a religious system that God had set to one side, to find in Christ alone the satisfying portion of their souls.

It will be observed that after each unfolding of truth, the Spirit of God gives a special warning lest having heard with the outward ear, the truth may not have entered the heart, and there may be a slipping away from it. This will result in a drifting back to a religious system that has nothing to offer a sinner seeking a purged conscience and desiring to enter into the presence of God in peace. These warnings had special application to the Hebrews of apostolic days who had heard the gospel and were intellectually convinced that Jesus was the promised Messiah. They were however in danger of mistaking outward adherence to His cause for heart-acceptance of Christ as their Savior, even as many do today. It is quite possible to believe the Scripture records, accept their historicity and acknowledge the messiahship of Jesus, with the conscience unexercised and no evidence of repentance unto life whatsoever. Therefore we see the importance of giving heed to the warnings as well as to the truth unfolded in this Epistle.

Professing Christians today are in no real sense in exactly the same position as those who in the first Christian centuries had turned away from Judaism and declared themselves followers of Jesus the Messiah. Because of the severe persecutions to which they were exposed, those early Christians were sorely tempted to recant and go back to the ancient religious system. Yet many in Christendom today take the place of being followers of our Lord and Savior, but in the hour of testing they are in grave peril because they have undervalued the great truths of the gospel. They never go further than a mere, intellectual acquiescence in the ethical precepts of Christianity, and know nothing of the new birth and the saving power of the blood of Christ. It is easy for these intellectual Christians to profess to hold what they are pleased to call the religion of Jesus while repudiating the atoning work of the cross and His high priestly intercession. Both of these teachings are of no value whatever unless Christ is what the Scriptures declare Him to be—the Son of God in all reality, as well as Son of man. "What think ye of Christ?" is still the great and abiding test.

As we study this Epistle together, may we indeed see in Christ the One who has fulfilled all the shadows of the legal dispensation. He is the satisfying portion of all who turn to Him as repentant sinners, trusting Him alone for their eternal redemption.

CHAPTER ONE

THE GLORY OF
THE SON OF GOD

As we begin our study of this sublime Epistle, we are brought face to face with God Himself, ever yearning for the love and confidence of the race created in His own image and after His own likeness. The first head of this race was scarcely placed in a position of authority before he departed from the Creator, obedience to whom ever means blessing, and disobedience, misery and remorse. Sin had no sooner come into the world than God came in grace seeking the sinner. So from the first question, "[Adam], where art thou?" (Genesis 3:9) on to the incarnation, God has been speaking to man.

God Speaking through the Son (1:1-4)

In many places and in many ways in former times, God made known His mind through divinely inspired men—prophets who spoke as they were moved by the Holy Spirit. But while in this way God was revealed in measure, that revelation could be, in the nature of things, only fragmentary.

Now in the fullness of times, at the end of the probationary ages, in these days of blessing He has spoken to us not through a mere human agency, but in the person of the Son. In other words, it is not now God sending a messenger to man to make known His will and to call him back to Himself, but it is God coming out to man in the Son. This is the same as that of which the apostle John wrote: "And the Word was made flesh, and dwelt among us, (and we beheld his glory, the glory as of the only begotten of the Father,) full of grace and truth....No man hath seen God at any time; the only begotten Son, which is in the bosom of the Father, he hath declared him" (John 1:14,18). God is no longer hidden nor at a distance. He has come down into His own world seeking those who have wandered from Him. He has revealed Himself in all His infinite holiness and righteousness and yet with all His matchless love and compassion. In Christ, God is fully told out. None need say now, "Oh, that I knew where I might find Him!" or, "Show us the Father and it sufficeth us." For the eternal Son who became flesh to make God known has said, "He that hath seen me hath seen the Father" (John 14:9), and "I and my Father are one" (10:30).

It is of all importance that we grasp this tremendous fact. The Son is one with the Father and with the Spirit. All are coequal and coeternal. When the Son became incarnate, He was the same person that He had been from eternity, but by His incarnation He took humanity into union with deity and so became Son in a new sense as man born of a virgin. Having no human father, God alone was the Father of His humanity as truly as of His deity. I admit the awkwardness of the last expression, but this is a mystery almost unlawful for man to utter, and of necessity our poor language is a most imperfect vehicle to convey to the mind such sublime truths. Yet there can be no questioning of the truths for one who accepts the testimony of the Word of God.

God has established the Son as heir of all things (Hebrews 1:2). This refers to Him as having become man, for it is as man He will rule a redeemed universe in righteousness. But the apostle immediately adds, "By whom also he made the worlds," and this brings us face to face with God Himself, God the Creator of all things. The same person who made the universe will reign over it. It is interesting to note that the word translated "worlds" (KJV) is literally "ages" (*tous aionas*). This expression actually means the "time worlds" and was frequently translated the "universe." Perhaps it might be correct to say, "By Him also the ages were fitted together;" that is, Christ the Son is the center of all God's thoughts, and it is He who planned the ages and who created the world in which the dispensations would be manifested.

He is the forth-shining of the divine splendor, or the effulgence of His glory. J. N. Darby, in commenting on this word "effulgence," speaks of it as that which fully presents the glory that is in something else, as light makes us know what the sun is; the tabernacle, what the pattern in the mount was. So when we become acquainted with the Lord Jesus as set before us in the Gospels, we learn what God is in all His fullness. For Christ is the exact expression of His character, or as we have it in the King James version, "the express image of his person" (1:3). The divine character is perfectly revealed in the man Christ Jesus.

This truth is the very opposite to the modern thought of an apotheosis. Jesus was not a godlike man, striving after holiness and piety. He was God Himself come down to earth in flesh, reconciling the world unto Himself. Nothing like this is known in any human religious system. It is unique because it is divine, and divine because it is unique. Man could easily think of becoming God. This was the devil's lie at the beginning, "Ye shall be as *Elohim*," and is the foundation principle of all false religious systems. In Christianity alone do we learn that God became man, and this for our redemption.

He who was crucified through weakness was the One who, at that very moment, was "upholding all things by the word of his power." Never for one instant did He take His hand off the control bar of the universe. What a marvelous suggestion of power there is in these words, and how our thoughts of Him are magnified as we realize who it was who stooped in grace to make purification of sins!

We read, "He had by himself purged our sins." It is evident that the King James version does not quite give the accurate thought here, for there are many whose sins are not purged. The Epistle to the Hebrews clearly takes this into account. The words "by himself" are not found in the original at all, but they are implied because the verb is in the middle voice, which reflects the action back upon the subject. On the other hand, the word "our" must be omitted altogether. It is the act of making an available means for purgation that is here stressed, "Having accomplished the purification of sins (by Himself)." That is, upon the cross He finished the work whereby the sin question is settled to the divine satisfaction. That question, as such, no longer comes up between God and men, but all who trust in Him are, upon the basis of Christ's work, actually purified or purged from all their sins before God.

This work having been completed, He took His seat as man on the right hand of the eternal Majesty on high. None but a divine person could sit on the throne of the universe. But there He sits as entitled to share that throne with His Father. And He is there, be it observed, as man in a glorified body, but a real body nevertheless. He is in the same body that was nailed to the cross and that lay in Joseph's tomb, but now transfigured as when His disciples beheld Him on the holy mount.

> Now seated on Jehovah's throne,
> The Lamb once slain, in glory bright,
> 'Tis thence Thou watchest o'er Thine own,
> Guarding them through the deadly fight.

So by taking this place, He has made it clear that His is a name far more excellent than that of any created angel (1:4). They are but ministers and servants. He is Son. Here for the first time we get the word *better*, a term that occurs frequently in this Epistle as already indicated. The Son is so much better than the angels because by inheritance He has a name superior to their names. It is not what He wins by His devotedness, it is that which is His by right because of His relationship to the Father from eternity.

The Son Greater than the Angels (1:5-14)

In these verses the apostle proceeded to marshal an array of Old Testament scriptures to show the superiority of the Son to the angels. The author also proved, particularly to those who like his Jewish readers reverence the Old Testament, that He is not teaching anything contrary to what was therein revealed.

Let us look at these scriptures in order. The first one gives us His incarnation (1:5). The quotation is from Psalm 2:7: "Thou art my Son; this day have I begotten thee." The expression "this day" forbids the thought that it is eternal generation that is here referred to, true as that is. It is as begotten of the virgin that the Father addressed Him as Son. I know it is sometimes said that the reference is to His resurrection, based on the King James reading of Acts 13:33, where we read, "He hath raised up Jesus again; as it is also written in the second psalm, ..." But the word *again* is an interpolation as any carefully edited text would show. It is simply, He has raised up Jesus, in accordance with the words, "Thou art my Son, this day have I begotten thee," thus agreeing perfectly with the angel's message to the blessed virgin Mary: "That holy thing which shall be born of thee shall be called the Son of God" (Luke 1:35).

In the second quotation we have His walk of faith here upon the earth: "I will be to him a Father, and he shall be to me a Son" (1:5). This is evidently the promise made to David as recorded in 2 Samuel 7:14 and celebrated in Psalm 89. At first sight, it might seem to have reference to Solomon, but it is evident that a greater than Solomon was in view—He who even from His childhood could say, "Wist ye not that I must be about my Father's business?" (Luke 2:49)

The third quotation (Hebrews 1:6) is taken from Psalm 97:7, where it is rendered in the King James version, "Worship him, all ye gods." This Psalm celebrates Messiah's triumph over the enemies of Jehovah and His appearing in glory to reign over all the nations. The reference is clearly, I take it, to His second coming. It is not exactly, "When He *brought* His first begotten into the world," but "when He *brings*" Him again into the inhabited earth. In that day all will recognize Him as the supreme object of worship. In contrast to this, it is said of the angels in Psalm 104:4, "Who maketh his angels spirits; his ministers a flaming fire." They are created beings, and never occupy any other place than that of servants.

The next two verses (Hebrews 1:8-9) are taken from Psalm 45, where in verse 6 we have before us the eternal Son, and in verse 7 the Son become man. In the first instance He is directly addressed by the Father as God from eternity: "Unto the Son he saith, thy throne, O God, is forever and ever; a sceptre of righteousness is the sceptre of thy kingdom." He is called directly "The God" (*Ho Theos*). It would be impossible to indicate His full deity in any more conclusive way than this. But the next verse shows that Christ has walked through this world as man displaying the divine character—loving righteousness and hating iniquity. And as man, God is His God and has now anointed Him with the oil of gladness above His companions.

The next quotation (1:10-12) requires most careful attention in order not to miss the force of it. It is taken from Psalm 102:25-27. In verses 23 and 24 of that Psalm, the Son is heard addressing the Father in view of the cross. He cries, "He weakened my strength in the way; he shortened my days. I said, O my God, take me not away in the midst of my days: thy years are throughout all generations." The verses that follow might seem at first glance to be a continuation of His plea, but with the light that the Epistle of Hebrews throws on them, we see that they are the answer of the Father to the Son. God replies to the sufferer of Calvary:

> Of old hast thou laid the foundation of the earth: and the heavens are the work of thy hands. They shall perish, but thou shalt endure: yea, all of them shall wax old like a garment; as a vesture shalt thou change them, and they shall be changed: But thou art the same, and thy years shall have no end (Psalm 102:25-27).

Thus the apostle has established the full deity of our blessed Lord in contrast with whom angels, however glorious, are but creatures. They are ministering spirits sent forth to minister to them who shall be heirs of salvation, and who themselves worship the Son of God (1:14).

CHAPTER TWO

THE SUFFERINGS OF THE SON OF MAN

Having considered our blessed Lord from the standpoint of His deity, both as the eternal Son and as the Son of God in manhood, we are now called upon to think of Him in His humiliation. He entered into the experiences of humanity in order that He might become the Captain of our salvation. We should never forget that His humanity is as real as His deity. He was born of a virgin; to all outward appearances He was a baby like any other, and a perfectly normal child. He grew from infancy to manhood, increasing in wisdom as He increased in stature, and was a sharer in all that pertained to human nature as originally created by God. And He has gone up to Heaven as man, so that we may properly sing, "He wears our nature on the throne."

But let us never forget His human nature was sinless throughout as was that of Adam before the fall. He did not come under Adam's federal headship and so did not inherit his fallen estate. God alone was His Father, as we have already seen, and as Scripture abundantly bears witness. Inasmuch as He was both God and man in one person, His humanity was not only innocent as was that of the first man, which was therefore subject to failure, but it was holy. Christ's humanity repelled evil, for He was the second man, the Lord from Heaven. This precludes all possibility of sin or failure on His part.

Nevertheless, He entered into our human condition and circumstances, not when the race was unfallen but after the fall, when it had become bruised and battered by sin. So as sinless man He passed through this life exposed to pain and sorrow, to hunger and weariness, to trial and temptation, and entered fully into all human experiences that did not involve personal demerit. He died at last on a felon's cross where Jehovah laid upon Him the iniquity of us all. While there was no sin in Him, our sins were placed upon Him, and He made full expiation for all our iniquities that we might be reconciled to God and justified from all things.

Warning to Heed the Truth (2:1-4)

In these verses we have a solemn warning addressed to all who have received the truth of Christ's superiority to angels. The readers are exhorted to give earnest attention to this truth lest at any time it should drift past them. It is one thing to accept the truth intellectually and profess adherence to certain doctrines. It is another thing to receive the truth in the heart and thus to be born of God. The danger for these Hebrews was that they might have allied themselves with the Christian company outwardly while never having actually received the truth in their hearts, by which means alone they could be regenerated. There was always the danger that under the stress of persecution such professors might give up or drift away from what was of prime importance—a true confession of Christ.

"The word spoken by angels," referred to in verse 2, is the law of old. The readers of Hebrews were warned that just as when God gave the law, "every transgression and disobedience received a just recompense of reward," even though the people had declared their adherence to it; so now, "how shall we escape" if we are careless regarding so great salvation? Our salvation is great because of the dignity of the person who accomplished it. It was first proclaimed by the Lord Himself when here in the world, and later confirmed by His apostles (3). God had set His seal to their testimony by giving them the power to work mighty signs and wonders, as promised in Mark 16 and elsewhere. These signs followed them as they went everywhere preaching the Word. The Holy Spirit worked miraculously through them to accredit the gospel message (4). To turn away from Christianity would mean to blaspheme against the Holy Ghost, for one cannot reject the testimony thus accredited without denying the work of the Holy Spirit. If the mighty signs were not wrought by Him, who then was their author? The Jewish readers of this Epistle must acknowledge that the Holy Spirit was bearing witness to the truth of the gospel, or, as their fathers had done, impute these wonders to the power of Satan.

Notice that the gifts of the Spirit were according to His own will. This is important, and it is in accord with what is written in 1 Corinthians 12:11, concerning spiritual gifts: "But all these worketh that one and the selfsame Spirit, dividing to every man severally as he will." If this were better understood, there would be less insistence on certain gifts as evidences of the Spirit's indwelling.

The Glory and Authority of the Son (2:5-9)

While angels are greater in power and might than man in his present circumstances, they remain but servants. It was never God's purpose that the angels should be rulers over humanity. During the present age and throughout past dispensations, God has been pleased to use angels as His messengers in conveying His will to man. These glorious beings appeared to the patriarchs either to announce blessing or to warn of judgment. The law was given by the disposition of angels. The people of Israel were led by angelic guidance through the wilderness, and during all the years of the theocracy angels appeared from time to time as representatives of the throne of God. When our blessed Lord Himself was here on earth angels came to minister to Him, and when He comes into the world again, as we have seen in Hebrews 1, they will all worship Him. But it is not in the plan of God that they should administer the affairs of the divine government when the kingdom is actually established.

"Unto the angels hath he not put in subjection the [age] to come" (2:5). Notice it is *age,* not *world.* The writer did not have the cosmos in view, but the coming age of righteousness when the kingdoms of this world will become the kingdoms of our Lord and of His Christ. No angel will rule in that day. But He whose glory was foretold in Psalm 8 will take the kingdom and rule in righteousness, for the "certain place" referred to in Hebrews 2:6 is, as we know, Psalm 8:4-6:

What is man, that thou art mindful of him? and the son of man, that thou visitest him? For thou hast made him a little lower than the angels, and hast crowned him with glory and honour. Thou madest him to have dominion over the works of thy hands; thou hast put all things under his feet.

If we turn back to the Psalm we might not realize that it is Christ who is in view, particularly as we notice verses 7 and 8 where all cattle and wild beasts, as well as fowls of the air and the fish of the sea, are said to be subjected to man. It might look as though it is but a confirmation of the Lord's word to Adam the first. God had said to Adam, "Be fruitful, and multiply, and replenish the earth, and subdue it: and have dominion over the fish of the sea, and over the fowl of the air, and over every living thing that moveth upon the earth" (Genesis 1: 28). But we know well that Adam forfeited his headship through sin, and in Psalm 8 that headship was confirmed to One who is called the Son of man, which Adam never was. The apostle's use of Psalm 8 in Hebrews 2 makes it plain that it is the last Adam to whom the Psalm refers. And so, as we read these words, we think of Christ who delighted in the title "Son of man" because it speaks of Him as the appointed ruler over the whole earth. He is to deliver it from the bondage of corruption.

He was made a little lower than the angels—that is, He became man, and men in their present condition are inferior to angels. When redemption is completed, we shall have a place higher than angels can ever aspire to. And already He who took that place of humility has been received up into Heaven as man and crowned with glory and honor, and by divine fiat set over all creation. For God has appointed Him heir of all things and decreed that all will be in subjection under His feet. He leaves nothing unsubjected to Him. His place is that of supreme authority.

But as we look around the world today, can we think for a moment that His authority is being exercised? "We see not yet all things put under him" (2:8). Though many centuries have passed since this Epistle to the Hebrews was written, rebellion against God still characterizes this lower universe. The divine law is flouted. The grace of God is despised. His Word is refused. His Holy Spirit is ignored. His people are still called to suffer for righteousness' sake. Surely all things are not yet put under Him! Such might well be the natural conclusion to which we would come if we looked only on the things that are seen.

But when we pierce the heavens with the eye of faith, through the telescope of the Word, we see Jesus, who once became a little lower than the angels with the view to the suffering of death, even now crowned with glory and honor. He sits exalted on the throne of the eternal God as a glorified man at the right hand of the Majesty on high. God has set Him above all things, which is conclusive proof to us that all things shall yet be subjected to Him.

Notice the special reason given for His humiliation. He became "a little lower than the angels for the suffering of death"—that is, with this very object in view (9). It was impossible that deity as such should die. If He would taste death for every man, He must become man, for only as man could He die. This is the mystery illustrated in that ancient type in Leviticus 14:5 where, in connection with the cleansing of the leper, the priest was instructed to take two birds alive and clean. One of the birds was to be killed in an earthen vessel over running water. The other was to be dipped in the blood of the dead bird and let loose in the open field. The two birds typified one Christ. The first bird symbolized Him as the heavenly One who entered into the earthen vessel of humanity in order that He might die. The second bird speaks of Him as the risen One who has returned to the heavens in all the value of His own most precious blood.

Then it is well to notice that after all it is not merely for every man that He tasted death. The context makes it plain that the "all" for which He died is in the neuter in the original. It might rightly be rendered, "that He by the grace of God should taste death for everything." For through His death not only will sinners be saved and the world of redeemed men brought into eternal blessing, but the creation itself will be delivered from the bondage of corruption. Everything in Heaven and earth will at last be brought into harmony with God. None shall fail of this reconciliation excepting those who deliberately prefer their sins to the salvation so freely offered.

Perfection of the Son through Suffering (2:10-18)

This section is one of the most precious in all the Epistle and requires careful consideration. There is grave danger of misunderstanding some of its great declarations unless we are familiar with what the Word of God elsewhere reveals concerning the person and work of the Lord Jesus.

If He would become Captain of our salvation (literally, File leader of our salvation), the One who is Himself the Way of Life and leads us in that Way, He must be perfected through sufferings. But notice how His glory as Creator is insisted on when His sufferings are in view. Let us take a closer look at verse 10. "It became him"—that is, it was consistent under the circumstances for Him; "for whom are all things and by whom are all things"—the same as in Colossians 1:16, "All things were created by him, and for him"; "in bringing many sons unto glory"—and this we know is the very reason for which He came into the world; "to make the captain of their salvation perfect"—not as to His character, but as to His saviorhood— "through sufferings." There was never any imperfection in Him as man. He was always the perfect One, but let it never be forgotten that the perfect life of Jesus would never have saved one poor sinner. In order to become Captain of salvation that He might lead many sons to glory, He must go by way of Gethsemane and Golgotha where He was perfected by sufferings. Apart from His bitter passion, there could be no redemption for lost men and women.

In verse 11 we have the glorious result of His sufferings: "Both he that sanctifieth and they who are sanctified are all of one." To sanctify is to separate, to set apart. He set Himself apart in order that He might become our Savior. "For their sakes I sanctify myself, that they also might be sanctified through the truth" (John 17:19). And now as having returned to the glory from whence He came, He is Himself the sanctifier of all His own. He has been "made unto us wisdom, and righteousness, and sanctification, and redemption"

(1 Corinthians 1:30). Every believer has been set apart by Him and in Him to God the Father, and so it can be said of Him and of us, we "are all of one." That is, we are all of one Father or of one family. And therefore He is not ashamed to call us brethren. Our poor hearts cannot but realize how worthless we have been and are. If He were any other than He is, He might well be ashamed to acknowledge us as His brethren. But we have become partakers of His divine life, a life that is eternal and to which sin can never attach. And so He owns us gladly as His brethren, though nowhere in Scripture is He spoken of as our brother. He said, "Ye call me Master and Lord, and ye say well, for so I am" (John 13:13). But He whom we gladly own as Lord, in wondrous grace calls us His brothers.

In Psalm 22 we see Him hanging on the cross, the forsaken One, drinking the wormwood and the gall, bearing the judgment due to our sins. In verses 1-21 of that Psalm He is seen alone, suffering at the hands of God what our guilt deserved. Then from verse 22 on He is no longer alone, but as the risen One He is surrounded by multitudes who owe their salvation to His sufferings on the tree. In resurrection He exclaims: "I will declare thy name unto my brethren; in the midst of the congregation will I praise thee." This is the passage that is quoted in Hebrews 2:12; but for *congregation* we have the word *church,* a translation of the Greek *ekklesia.* This was the Septuagint rendering for the Hebrew term translated "congregation." It is the assembly of the redeemed, and in the midst of that assembly the risen Christ takes His place as the chief chorister leading the praises of His people's hearts.

He once trod the path of faith Himself, as implied in the quotation in verse 13 from Isaiah 8:17, "I will put my trust in him." As man here on earth, He walked through the wilderness of this world with perfect confidence in the Father. He looked on to the time when, surrounded by all His own, He could say, as quoted from Isaiah 8:18, "Behold, I and the children which God hath given me." But it is not to Isaiah and his children that these words primarily apply. The prophet was but the type of the Lord Himself who spoke by the Spirit through Isaiah.

It is necessary to give the most careful consideration to Hebrews

2:14-15 lest we, even though unintentionally, detract from the glory of the humanity of our blessed Lord. A casual reading of the first part of verse 14 might suggest that our Savior participated in everything that is connected with flesh and blood. Indeed, this has been the teaching of many. According to them, the Son of God assumed humanity with all its sinfulness and all its limitations of ignorance. Even though they acknowledge that in some sense He was truly God revealed in flesh, yet with them it is deity enshrouded in poor degraded sinful human nature and therefore unable to make Himself known in His fullness. But what we are really told here is that inasmuch as the children of faith are human beings, not angels, as the writer points out in verse 16, so in order that He might be the true *goel* or kinsman-redeemer, He in infinite grace became man and thus took part of the same human nature. This does not in any sense imply that He took defiled human nature. The Holy Spirit guarded against this in the fullest possible way, so that the angel could say to Mary, "That holy thing which shall be born of thee shall be called the Son of God." While in our English version the words "partakers of" and "took part of" might seem to imply in each instance fullest participation, the original does not necessarily imply this. The following note from the pen of the spiritual expositor F. W. Grant is very helpful.

> It must be noted here, as it often has been, that while the children are said to be partakers of flesh and blood—this "partaking" being a real having in common, a participation of the most thorough kind—in His own "taking part" another word is used which implies limitation. It does not indeed show the character of the limitation; but the difference between the words makes us necessarily ask what, in fact, that [limitation] was; and the answer comes to us immediately, that while His was true humanity in every particular necessary to constitute it that, yet humanity as men have it, the humanity of *fallen* men, was *not* His. Here there must be strict limitation. We must add, as the apostle does afterwards with regard to His temptation, "sin apart." Sin, with the consequences of sin, He could not take. Death could have no power over Him, except as He might

submit Himself voluntarily to it, and this He did; but it was obedience to His Father's will, and no necessity of His condition, as it is of ours (*Numerical Bible,* Volume 7, Neptune NJ: Loizeaux, 1902, page 23).

We must remember that sin is not inherent in human nature as such, but that it is a foreign thing brought in through the fall. Then we can readily understand how it could be said that our blessed Lord "took part of the same" without involving full participation in all that had come in through man's failure. He must be the unblemished One if He would make satisfaction for sins. It is through failure to realize this that many very wrong systems have been built up teaching the sinfulness of Christ's humanity, something which one would expect would be repugnant to every truly converted person.

Having thus become man, though sinless, our Lord became man's champion and went forth as our David to destroy or annul the great Goliath who had terrorized the world ever since the fall—"him that had the power of death, that is, the devil" (2:14). The cross was for Christ a valley of Elah where He met our cruel foe and put an end to his authority over the souls of all who believe the gospel. Thereby He delivered us even now, who in times past through fear of death were held in bitter bondage all our lives. Satan is a conquered foe and no believer need now fear him. But it is incumbent on us to watch and pray lest he mislead us and hinder our communion with God, though he well knows he can never destroy our life.

The sixteenth verse seems to be unfortunately rendered in the King James version by the insertion of the italicized words, which imply that it is a question of nature that is under consideration. A better translation reads as follows: "For truly He taketh not hold of angels, but of the seed of Abraham He took hold." That is, Christ did not come to be the Savior of fallen angels. They are shut up unto eternal darkness, but in infinite grace He passed angels by and laid hold on the seed of Abraham—that is, on all who believe in Him. In order to help Abraham's descendants it was necessary that He should be made like unto His brethren, that thus having passed sinlessly through all human experiences, He might be a merciful and faithful High Priest in things pertaining to God (17). He made not *reconciliation,* as in the King James version text, but *expiation* or *atonement* for the sins of the people. In this we see the fulfillment of the type of the great day of atonement when the high priest first offered the sacrifice at the altar and then presented the blood in the holiest. So our Lord, at the close of His pilgrim path, on our behalf offered up Himself on the cross to make atonement for our sins. The original word is that used in the Septuagint version of the Old Testament to translate the Hebrew word for atonement. Reconciliation is the result of this, but it is we who are reconciled to God, not He who has to be reconciled to us.

And now our Great High Priest lives on high ever ready to help them that are tempted. Having Himself suffered being tempted, His heart goes out in compassion to us in our great need. Note the contrast between Hebrews 2:17-18 and 1 Peter 4:1. In Hebrews we read that Christ "suffered being tempted." In the other passage we are told that "He that suffered in the flesh hath ceased from sin." This brings out most vividly the difference between Christ's perfect humanity and our sinful natures. To us, sin is attractive and alluring. We suffer in the flesh when we resist it. With Him it was the very opposite. Temptation caused Him the keenest suffering. He abhorred the very presentation of sin to His holy soul, and even to have to deal with it, in the sense of temptation, caused Him pain and anguish.

CHAPTER THREE
THE GLORY OF THE SON OVER THE HOUSE OF GOD

Having introduced Christ Jesus as High Priest of our confession, we are now bidden to consider Him as the Apostle of the new dispensation.

Jesus Greater than Moses (3:1-6)

Christ has superseded both Moses and Aaron. Moses was the apostle of the separated people who were partakers of an earthly calling, and Aaron was their high priest. But Jesus is both the Apostle and High Priest of the holy brethren. They are holy because they are set apart to God in Christ, and thus partakers of the heavenly calling.

He is infinitely superior to Moses because Moses, though faithful in his day, was simply a servant in the house of God, but Christ Jesus is the Builder of the house. He is also Son over His own house, "whose house are we, if we hold fast the confidence and the rejoicing of the hope firm unto the end" (6). Observe that the term *house* is used here in three senses. The house in which Moses was faithful was the tabernacle (2,5). But the tabernacle was the pattern of things in the heavens, so the house that God built is the universe (3-4). But the house over which Christ is set and to which we belong is that building composed of living stones in which every believer has a place (6).

In verse 6 we have the first word of warning, lest in cherishing a temporary confidence we seem to be animated by the joy that hope in Christ gives, and yet are lacking in genuine faith. The *if* in this verse is a test of profession. It was very possible then, and it is still, that men might mingle with a Christian company and find a certain amount of gladness and joy springing from an intellectual acquaintance with Christianity, who after all are not truly born of God. Continuance proves the reality of our confession. This is further stressed in the portion that follows.

Warning Against Unbelief (3:7-19)

In this section the warning is continued and is based on Israel's experiences in the past. Just as their fathers had left Egypt a great multitude, yet many (in fact, the majority) failed to enter the land of Canaan because of unbelief; so a vast throng of Jews had become outwardly obedient to the faith, but there was ever the danger that their conversion to Christianity might be merely intellectual. Their forsaking of Judaism might simply have been what people sometimes call today "a change of religion." Therefore the importance of examining themselves in the light of the Word of God and pressing on to "make [their] calling and election sure," as the apostle Peter puts it in 2 Peter 1:10. We are saved entirely by grace, but we are created in Christ Jesus unto good works, as we read in Ephesians 2:10. No one has a right to confess himself a Christian who is not seeking to live for the glory of God. There is every reason to doubt the salvation of one whose nature does not delight in the will of God.

And so we have here a warning word taken from Psalm 95:7-11:

> For he is our God; and we are the people of his pasture, and the sheep of his hand. To day if ye will hear his voice, Harden not your heart, as in the provocation, and as in the day of temptation in the wilderness: When your fathers tempted me, proved me, and saw my work. Forty years long was I grieved with this generation, and said, It is a people that do err in their heart, and they have not known my ways: Unto whom I sware in my wrath that they should not enter into my rest.

Notice how this quotation from the Psalm is introduced in Hebrews, "As the Holy Ghost saith" (3:7). It is not merely the word of David or some other unknown author. It is the word of the Holy Spirit Himself warning those who profess the name of the Lord against hardening their hearts and walking in disobedience.

To these Hebrews the exhortation is given:

> Take heed, brethren, lest there be in any of you an evil heart of unbelief, in departing from the living God. But exhort one another daily, while it is called To day; lest any of you be hardened through the deceitfulness of sin. For we are made partakers [companions] of Christ, if we hold the beginning of our confidence stedfast unto the end (12-14).

Faith is manifested by a godly walk. Where there is lack of faith, the outward life may for a time seem to be consistent with the Christian profession, but eventually the old carnal nature will assert itself and there will be a turning back to the world. Or, as in the case with the Hebrews, they may have returned to that mere carnal religion from which Christ would deliver. The second *if* (14) is linked with verse 6, and again we are reminded that continuance in the walk of faith is the proof of a genuine Christian confession.

In the last five verses of Hebrews 3, the Spirit of God used the case of Israel in the wilderness as a solemn warning to all who now have professedly gone on a pilgrimage. The Israelites who fell in the desert were those who did not believe. They never entered into God's rest. Indeed, they could not do so because of their unbelief. That rest of course was Canaan, a type of the rest that remains for the people of God now.

CHAPTER FOUR
THE ETERNAL SABBATH OF GOD

There are those today who deny utterly Christ's priestly service on behalf of the church. They say (to use the exact language of one of the teachers of this school), "Christ is not my High Priest; He is a High Priest for Israel, not for the church which is His body. All believers now are part of the High Priest and it will be our place to intercede for Israel by and by." What an absurd obsession must he be laboring under who can use such language! Christ as the Head of the body, the church, is one aspect in which our blessed Lord is presented in the Word, but Christ as the High Priest is another aspect altogether. As members of the body we are seen in a peculiar relationship to Him, which does not involve the thought of failure or infirmity. But as a pilgrim people passing through a sinful world, we have a Great High Priest ever representing us before God in Heaven and ministering to our needs as they arise from moment to moment. To rob the Christian of this blessed truth is to leave him poor indeed. But that teaching is just part of an ultra-dispensational system which is soul-withering in the extreme, and occupies its followers with fine distinctions that are often thoroughly unscriptural, instead of with Christ Himself and His work on our behalf.

Warning of Coming Short of the Eternal Rest (4:1-13)

Before writing of the high priesthood of Christ, the apostle continued the subject of the eternal rest. "Let us therefore fear, lest a promise being left us of entering into his rest, any of you should

51

seem to come short of it" (1). The *rest* here spoken of is not our present enjoyment of Christ, as many have imagined, but clearly refers to that rest which, as in Israel's case, is at the end of the way. What a solemn thing for any who eventually come short of that! We have heard the glad tidings of a rest to come, as did the Israelites. Let us then see that we profit thereby in a way which they did not, proving the reality of our faith by our behavior.

In verse 3 the apostle wrote of the present rest we have as we truly believe God and enjoy the rest of faith. The quotation from Psalm 95 is again referred to in order to show that the rest there spoken of could not refer merely to creation rest, for God entered into that centuries and millenniums before the Psalm was written, as we read in Genesis 2:2: "[God] rested on the seventh day from all his work." But the Psalm says, "They should not enter into my rest," showing that the rest was still future. Nor was it merely Canaan rest, for they had long since reached Canaan, though those who did not believe failed of this. But another and a better rest is before the mind of the Spirit, for if Joshua had given them rest, God would not have spoken as though their rest was still in the future.

It is well known that the name of our blessed Lord which we read as *Jesus*, is the Greek form of the Hebrew *Joshua*. Therefore Israel's great leader and our great Savior both bore the same name. Joshua led those who believed into Canaan rest. Jesus leads those who believe into the present rest of faith and later into eternal rest. Both are brought before us in verses 9-11: "There remaineth therefore a rest to the people of God. For he that is entered into his rest, he also hath ceased from his own works, as God did from his. Let us labor therefore to enter into that rest, lest any man fall after the same example of unbelief." Verse 9 refers to an eternal rest, a sabbath keeping that will have no end, whereas verse 10 speaks of that rest which we now enter into and enjoy as "we walk by faith and not by sight." We are exhorted to be in earnest lest we even so much as seem to fall short of what is our proper portion in Christ.

We need to remember that God's Word is ever the standard of judgment, and not our knowledge of it. Therefore the importance of becoming thoroughly conversant with the truth revealed in the holy Scriptures. In verses 12-13 we cannot but notice how intimately the written Word and the eternal Word are linked together. It is clear that verse 12 is referring to revealed truth. This is the Word of God that is described as living and energetic, "sharper than any twoedged sword, piercing even to the dividing asunder of soul and spirit"—that is, distinguishing between these two parts of the inward man. It also separates between the joints and marrow, making a difference between what is outward and that which is hidden. It "is a discerner [*kritikos*] of the thoughts and intents of the heart." Men presume to criticize and to sit in judgment on the Word of God, but here we are told that the Word itself is the supreme critic of our inmost thoughts and inclinations. Throughout verse 12 it is the written Word that is in view, but in verse 13 we have the personal pronouns used, showing us that the living Word is now before the soul. He is the One from whom nothing is hidden but to whose all-seeing eyes everything is naked and open. How important that those who have to do with Him be real and true in all their ways.

Our Great High Priest in Glory (4:14-16)

We are now to consider the priesthood of Christ, a precious and wondrous theme meaning much for all believers during His present session at God's right hand in Heaven. Jewish believers could enter this subject with peculiar interest because of their former relationship to the earthly sanctuary and the high priesthood of Aaron and his sons.

The greater division that we now enter, extending from Hebrews 4:14 to 10:39, is by far the largest part of the Epistle, and opens up to us a vast system of precious truth, namely, the priesthood of the heavenly sanctuary, a priesthood far superior to the Aaronic system. It is not only superior because of the more excellent character of the Priest Himself, but because of the infinitely better sacrifice on which it rests—the offering of the body of Jesus Christ once for all on the cross for our sins.

Properly speaking, priesthood has to do with the Heavens. Our blessed Lord was anointed to fulfill three offices—those of prophet, priest, and king. While to a certain extent these offices overlap, yet generally speaking we may say that He was Prophet on earth, He is

Priest in Heaven, and He will reign as King when He returns in glory. This however is not to deny that He was just as truly the King when He presented Himself to Israel in the days of His flesh. He was rejected in that special character when they exclaimed, "We have no king but Caesar," thus fulfilling the expression in the parable, "We will not have this man to reign over us" (Luke 19:14). And so too it was as High Priest that He lifted up His eyes unto Heaven and offered that wonderful intercessory prayer recorded in John 17. And as High Priest fulfilling the type of the great day of atonement, He offered Himself to God as a sacrifice on our behalf. Then, too, we see Him in the role of Prophet when on Patmos Isle He appeared to the beloved apostle and gave him a marvelous revelation concerning things that must shortly come to pass.

The high priest of the Old Testament must of necessity be a man, one who could enter into the trials of his brethren. And so our Lord Jesus has already been demonstrated to be true man as well as very God, that He might thus enter practically into all the sorrows and difficulties of His people. This is emphasized for us in Hebrews 4:14–5:10.

Our Lord is spoken of as a Great High Priest, great in the dignity of His person and in the perfection of His character (4:14). He has passed into (or, literally, through) the heavens, as the high priest of the old covenant, after having sacrificed at the altar, passed through the court and the holy place into the holy of holies. So our blessed Lord, having died on the cross, has passed through the lower heavens which we call the atmosphere; has gone on through the stellar heavens, the created universe stretching through apparently illimitable space; and has risen up into the Heaven of heavens, the immediate dwelling place of God. There He has taken His seat as man on the eternal throne. There He sits exalted, Jesus the Son of God, the entire title speaking most blessedly of His humanity and divinity. In view of His session at God's right hand, we are encouraged to "hold fast our confession." It is generally recognized that this is a better translation than "profession." We may profess what is not true, but we confess what is real.

Our High Priest then is not One whose heart is indifferent to our circumstances; not One who cannot be touched with the feeling of our infirmities (15). He is as truly human as we, and in the days of His flesh He was tempted in all points like ourselves, though apart from sin. The expression, "yet without sin," has frequently been taken to mean, "yet without sinning," as though it simply implied that He did not fail when exposed to temptation. But a more accurate rendering would be "sin apart"—that is, His temptations were entirely from without. He was never tempted by inbred sin as we are. He could say, "The prince of this world cometh and hath nothing in me" (John 14:30). When we are tempted from without, we have a traitor within who ever seeks to open the door of the citadel to the enemy. But it was otherwise with Him. If any ask, How then could His temptations be as real as ours? let us remember that when temptation was first presented to Adam and Eve, they were sinless beings, but being merely human they yielded and plunged the race into ruin and disaster. Christ was not only innocent but holy, for He was God as well as man.

"In all points tempted" means of course that appeals were made to Him by Satan from the three standpoints whereby any of us can be tempted: "the lust of the flesh, the lust of the eyes, and the pride of life" (1 John 2:16). Tempted on these three points, Eve capitulated completely. "The woman saw that the tree was good for food"—the appeal to the lust of the flesh; "it was pleasant to the eyes"—the appeal to the lust of the eye; "and a tree to be desired to make one wise"—the appeal to the pride of life (Genesis 3:6). She failed on every point. To our Lord in the wilderness the same appeals were made. "Command this stone that it be made bread"—an appeal to fleshly desire; "The devil...shewed unto him all the kingdoms of the world in a moment of time"—the lust of the eye; then in the suggestion that our Lord should cast Himself down from the pinnacle of the temple to be borne up by angels before the wondering eyes of the populace, we have the appeal to the pride of life (Luke 4:1-12). But He met every suggestion of evil by the Word of God. And now as the enthroned conqueror, He sits exalted on the right hand of the Majesty on high, interceding for us. We are bidden to come boldly unto the throne of grace there to obtain mercy because of failure, and find suited grace for seasonable help when exposed to temptation (16).

CHAPTER FIVE
THE ENTHRONED PRIEST

As we begin Hebrews 5 we are reminded that the high priest was taken from among men and set apart to minister on their behalf in things having to do with God.

The Superior Priesthood (5:1-10)

The high priest was to present his brethren's gifts and sacrifices for sins. Note the distinction between gifts and sacrifices. On the cross our Lord presented the sacrifice for sins. In Heaven now, He offers our gifts of worship and praise.

The earthly priest, because himself a man and as infirm as any of his brethren, could have compassion on the ignorant and on those who wandered from the path of rectitude. Conscious of his own failures he had to offer a propitiatory sacrifice for himself as well as for the people. In this we see the superiority of our Great High Priest, who needed no offering for Himself, but gave Himself in love for others.

In verse 4 we are reminded that no man was entitled to constitute himself a high priest. He became such by divine call, as in the case of Aaron who was chosen of God and set apart for this high office. Even so, Christ did not make Himself High Priest, but God the Father recognized Him as such when He declared in the words of Psalm 2, "Thou art my Son, today have I begotten thee." His Priesthood, however, was not of the Levitical order but of a different character altogether, even as it is written in Psalm 110:4, "Thou art a priest for ever after the order of Melchisedec." We will see the full implications of this when we consider Hebrews 7. It is enough to point out here that Melchisedec was recognized as priest of the most high God centuries before the Levitical priesthood came into existence. The Levitical priesthood and the legal covenant with which it was connected had their place until the Son, who was to fulfill the Melchisedec type, should come.

In Hebrews 5:7-10 the Spirit again emphasizes the reality of Christ's manhood and His participation in all the sinless experiences of His people. "In the days of his flesh," when He was here on earth in human condition, He trod the path of faith and took the place of dependence on the Father. "He … offered up prayers and supplications," accompanied by "strong crying and tears, unto him that was able to save him [out of] death." Be it observed, He was not saved from dying nor did He ever pray to be saved from death, nor did He fear death, as some have said. He came into the world to die, for that very purpose; but He was brought up from death, being raised by the power of God. What a testimony those tears were to the reality of His manhood! Three times we read of His weeping. He wept at the grave of Lazarus as He contemplated the awful ravages that death had made, tears of loving sympathy. He wept as He looked upon Jerusalem and His prophetic soul saw the tribulations through which the devoted city must pass. And He wept in Gethsemane's garden as His holy soul shrank from drinking the cup of divine indignation against sin when He would hang on the cross. While the cup could not be averted, nevertheless He was heard because of His piety—that is, because of His godly fear, His reverence for the Father's will. And thus He who is the eternal Son who never knew what subjection meant, became man. As He walked the pilgrim path of suffering and rejection down here, He learned obedience by the things that He suffered. It is not that His will had to be subdued, but that from the moment when He assumed humanity He entered into new experiences. He who had always commanded learned practically what obedience meant.

And thus being perfected as the Captain of our salvation, He was saluted by God in resurrection as High Priest after the order of Melchisedec. He has become the author of eternal salvation unto all them who follow Him in the obedience of faith.

How carefully the Holy Ghost guards against the least suggestion of defilement in Christ's nature while insisting on the reality of
His humanity. Great indeed is the mystery of godliness, for He, the
Holy One, appeared in flesh. And now as the exalted Priest, He
enters into all the sorrows of His people, sympathizing with them
in all their infirmities. He does not sympathize with our sins,
and indeed we would not wish Him to, but He does feel for us in all
our weakness and is waiting to supply needed strength for every
trial.

Warning Against Apostasy (5:11-14)

We are now to consider one of those portions of the writings of
"our beloved brother Paul," as Peter called him, "in which are some
things hard to be understood, which they that are unlearned and
unstable wrest...unto their own destruction" (2 Peter 3:16). Probably there is no part of the Word of God that has stumbled imma-
ture and uninstructed Christians like Hebrews 5:11–6:20. Therefore the need of examining it with the utmost care.

The closing part of Hebrews 5 is plain enough. Immediately upon
bringing in the name of Melchisedec the apostle declared: "Of whom
we have many things to say, and hard to be uttered, seeing ye are
dull of hearing" (11). The truth of the Melchisedec priesthood of
our Lord Jesus would be most unpalatable to Jewish tastes, and
difficult to understand where one was under legalistic bondage. We
have only to consult the book of Acts, particularly the record of
Paul's last visit to Jerusalem, to realize how backward thousands of
Hebrew believers were in the years immediately preceding the destruction of the holy city and the setting aside of the temple ritual.
Those who ought to have been well able to teach others, because of
the length of time that had elapsed since their conversion, were themselves needing instruction in the most elementary truths of the Word
of God. They had not even grasped the distinction between Israel's
hopes that are earthly, and those of the church, which are heavenly.
Neither had they realized the transitory and shadowy character of
the Levitical economy in contrast with the permanency of the Christian revelation. They were ignorant of the first principles of the

oracles of God, still requiring milk and unable to digest strong meat (12). They were babes in the truth when they should have been mature believers. The time had come to insist on the setting aside of Judaism and going on to the full truth of Christianity. And so it is to this great step they are called as the sixth chapter opens.

CHAPTER SIX
RESTING IN GOD'S WORD

The exhortation of the Spirit in Hebrews 6 is not to leave earlier Christian experiences and go on to a deeper work of grace, as some put it. Neither is it to cease from being occupied with the elementary truths of Christianity and go on to deeper things. It is a call to leave the typical for the actual; the shadow for the substance; the partial revelation of Judaism (using this word in its very best sense) for the full unfolding of the truth of the new dispensation.

Moving on from Preliminary Principles (6:1-3)

Judaism is called "the principles of the doctrine of Christ" (1). This includes the entire Mosaic revelation, the teaching of the prophets, and the ministry of John the Baptist. "The law and the prophets were until John: since that time the kingdom of God is preached, and every man presseth into it" (Luke 16:16). In six items the Spirit of God epitomizes these preliminary principles whereby the godly in Israel were prepared for the coming of the Christ (Hebrews 6:1-2):

1. Repentance from dead works
2. Faith toward God
3. The doctrine of baptisms (literally, a teaching concerning ceremonial washings)
4. The laying on of hands (in connection with the sacrificial offerings)

   5. Resurrection of the dead
   6. Eternal judgment

In these principles we have all that was basic in the former dispensation.

Throughout the Old Testament and in the ministry of John the Baptist, the people were called to repentance from dead works and urged to put their faith in the God of Israel. Through the ceremonial baptisms or washings of the law (as in Hebrews 9:10,13) the people were taught the need of cleansing, in order that they might have fellowship with God. These ceremonies were a cleansing from physical defilement alone, "the putting away of the filth of the flesh," as Peter puts it (1 Peter 3:21).

The "laying on of hands" has no reference whatever either to the laying on of the apostles' hands for the reception of the Holy Spirit as in Acts 8:17, or to ordination to the Christian ministry, as many have supposed. There is no doctrine of the laying on of hands to be found anywhere in the New Testament. Practice and doctrine are not the same thing. But under the Levitical economy when the offerer laid his hands on the head of the sacrifice that was presented to God on his behalf, he was picturing a tremendous truth on which this Epistle strongly insists. It was the identification of the offerer with the victim, and practically involved the transference of the offerer's sins to the offering that was put to death in the place of the sinner.

"Resurrection of the dead" is a cardinal Old Testament doctrine, denied indeed by worldly-minded Sadducees, but insisted on by the Pharisees. It was recognized by the apostle Paul as eminently scriptural, when he declared himself in this respect still a Pharisee after he had been converted to Christ for many years (Acts 23:6-8).

"Eternal judgment" is also part of the former revelation. "God shall bring every work into judgment, with every secret thing, whether it be good, or whether it be evil" (Ecclesiastes 12:14).

Now let us note the contrast between these six items and the outstanding truths of Christianity:

1. Repentance toward God (Acts 20:21)
2. Faith in our Lord Jesus Christ (Acts 20:21)
3. The cleansing of the conscience from dead works to serve the living and true God by the washing of regeneration and renewing of the Holy Ghost
4. The one offering of our Lord Jesus Christ with which every believer is fully identified
5. The out-resurrection from among the dead (Philippians 3:11, literal translation)
6. No judgment for the believer in Christ

Note how vividly the contrast is developed in the New Testament. The believer not only repents from dead works, but there is a complete change of attitude toward God. Faith is now in the Lord Jesus Christ definitely set forth as the sinner's only Savior. No outward cleansing will suffice; no washings with literal water or sprinkling of the blood of animal sacrifices. But cleansing from every sin by the precious blood of the Lord Jesus Christ and the washing of water by the Word applied in the Spirit's power is necessary. In place of the laying on of hands upon oft-repeated sacrifices, the believer can now say in the words of the well-known hymn:

> My faith would lay her hand
> On that blest head of Thine;
> While like a penitent I stand,
> And there confess my sin.
>
> My soul looks back to see
> The burden Thou didst bear,
> When hanging on th' accursed tree,
> And knows her guilt was there.

Also we have today the blessed unfolding of the truth that there are two resurrections; not as some put it, a general resurrection of the dead at the last day, but the resurrection from among the dead at the coming of our Lord Jesus Christ for all His own. And as to judgment we now know, or at least we should know, that the believer shall not come into judgment but has already passed out of death into life (John 5:24). It is then to this full unfolding of New Testament truth that these Hebrew believers were called to "go on" (Hebrews 6:1). This is Christianity, and Christianity is here designated as "perfection," distinguishing it from the imperfect or partial revelation of former days.

Warning Against Returning to Old Ways (6:4-9)

This, then, clears the way for the perplexing passage in verses 4 to 8. There were many Hebrews who in the beginning professed to acknowledge the messiahship of Jesus.They were eyewitnesses of the marvelous things that took place at Pentecost and afterwards. But as the Lord did not return and the promised kingdom was not immediately established, it was easy to understand how many of these, if lacking personal faith in Christ as Savior, would eventually give up the Messianic confession and go back to Judaism, which they knew to be a divinely revealed religion. This was a very serious thing. Yet this return to the old ways was something to which all these Hebrews would be exposed if they did not make a clean break with Judaism and go on to the perfection of Christianity. As to those who had already apostatized, it was too late to help them. They had made their choice and acted accordingly. Having experienced so much that was new and wonderful and then turned away from it all, they would be the hardest people on earth to change again.

It is impossible, we are told, to renew again to repentance those once enlightened (4-6). It is important to notice that the word *renew* does not imply, as J. N. Darby has pointed out, a renewal or change, but to make entirely new. This could never be true again of those who had given up their Christian profession. It is not a definite statement that there is no possible hope for the recovery of such, but it is a declaration that they could never now come into all the blessing of Christianity as a new thing. They had already tried it out, they would tell you, and had deliberately given it up. Such must be left with God, whereas those who really valued the truth were urged to press on to fuller knowledge.

Some object to the thought that anyone could go as far as these apostates had gone without being regenerated, but verse 9 is proof positive that such is the case. Notice the five things that are stated of these who had turned back.

1. They had been at one time enlightened as to the claims of Jesus the Messiah (4).
2. They had tasted the sweetness of the heavenly gift; this does not in itself imply that they had eaten of the living Bread (4).
3. They were made partakers of Holy Spirit (4). The definite article (*the*) is purposely omitted in the original. It was not that the Holy Spirit as a divine person had ever indwelt them, but they had participated in the blessing that the Spirit had given.
4. They had tasted the good Word of God, having listened to the good news of the gospel and to a certain extent appreciated the message that it brought (5).
5. They had been eyewitnesses of the works of power of the coming age, as were all who saw the mighty miracles done by our Lord and His apostles (5).

Now as we consider each one of these items separately it will, I think, become clear that all of these characteristics might be true of persons who had never experienced the regenerating grace of the Spirit of God.

Everyone who listens to the message of the new dispensation is thereby enlightened, for "the darkness is past, and the true light now shineth" (1 John 2:8). That light illuminates all who come under its gracious influence. But men may refuse the light and, by turning away from it, go back into darkness. How many there are who have been deeply stirred as they heard of the gift of God's Son and yet have never, like the Samaritan woman, judged themselves in the presence of the Lord and truly eaten this sacred food. To be a "partaker" of Holy Spirit is not at all the same thing as to be born of the Spirit, sealed by the Spirit, indwelt by the Spirit, anointed by the Spirit, baptized by the Spirit into the body of Christ, or filled with the Holy Spirit. It is simply to be made aware of the mighty power of the Spirit working on the hearts and minds of men bringing conviction, and wooing the heart toward Christ. One might tremble under this supernatural power and yet turn away from the message of the Spirit, which if truly believed would bring life and peace. Many, too, who have listened eagerly to the gospel, the good word of God, and have recognized to a certain extent the preciousness of the message, have failed to eat the Word. Jesus did not say, "he that tasteth of me shall live by me," but, "he that eateth me, even he shall live by me" (John 6:57). It is a definite act of faith that becomes a habit on life.

Then it is important to notice that the powers of the coming age (not "the world to come," merely) are the works that will characterize the return of our Lord and the millennial kingdom; in other words, miracles that were given as a sign to the Jews in order to authenticate the ministry of our Lord and His apostles. We read in John of many who believed on Him when they saw the signs that He did, yet who went back and walked no more with Him. And so it seems clear that these apostates were persons who had an outward acquaintance with Christianity but never knew what it was to receive the Lord Jesus as their own personal Savior. Definitely authenticated by works of power as He was, they still turned away from Him, and in so doing crucified for themselves the Son of God afresh, making a show of Him. This would be true of all who turned back from Christianity to Judaism.

In Hebrews 6:7-8 the apostle used a parable to make clear what was in his mind. He depicted two pieces of ground; both have been cultivated in the same way; both are warmed by the same sun; both drink in their share of the same rain. But one produces useful herbs for those who have farmed it, thus receiving a blessing from God. The other brings forth only the fruit of the curse—thorns and briars; it is worthless, and in danger of being completely given up when its good-for-nothing fruit is burned. What is the difference between these two pieces of ground? In the one case, you have good soil into which has fallen good seed. In the other, there is barren soil and the good seed has not fructified. The lesson is plain. Here are two Jews, let us say, who have been brought up side by side. Both have been interested in the law of Moses and the teachings of the prophets. Both have entertained the Messianic hope. Both have listened to the preaching of dedicated servants of Christ and have become deeply interested in the gospel. Both have been astounded at the mighty signs following the proclamation of the new message. Both make a profession of Christianity. Both are baptized and take their places in the Christian company. One of them bears the fruit of the Spirit in his life and becomes a devoted follower of the Savior. The other reveals no evidence of new life at all, and eventually repudiates Christianity and goes back to Judaism. He is not actually cursed as yet, for in the mercy of God he may eventually realize his fearful sin, but it is most unlikely. He has made his choice, and is therefore "nigh unto cursing." Now what is the difference between these two men? The one has truly turned to God in repentance, and the incorruptible seed of the gospel has fallen into the prepared soil of an honest upright heart. The other has become intellectually acquainted with and interested in Christianity, but the good seed has fallen on an unrepentant heart and has borne no fruit.

That we have not been mistaken in applying the passage in this way is definitely settled by the statement of verse 9. The apostle said, "But, beloved, we are persuaded better things of you, and things that accompany salvation, though we thus speak." They needed the warning and the urge to go on, but he was assured that those to whom he was addressing himself were truly saved people. If he saw in them better things than he had already described in verses 4-5, it is evident that one might have the experience of the privileges there enumerated and not have salvation.

Importance of Patient Persistence (6:10-20)

The proof of the reality of their faith was seen in their faithful service and love to fellow-saints leading to self-denying ministry (10). He desired them to show this gracious spirit to the end in the full assurance of hope. They were not to give way to slothfulness, but imitate those in past ages who, through faith and patience, became inheritors of the promise (11-12). He cited the case of their father Abraham to whom God sware by Himself, "Surely blessing I will bless thee, and multiplying I will multiply thee." But the promise was fulfilled only after Abraham had waited a long time (13-15). The word and oath of God were all that Abraham had for many years, but he held on in faith because he knew that God could not be untrue to His promise.

And so we too have strong encouragement to press on, counting on God. Like the manslayer of the old covenant who fled to the city of refuge, we have fled to God for refuge (Numbers 35:11). We lay hold of the hope set before us—that is, the hope of final and eternal salvation through our Lord Jesus Christ (Hebrews 6:18). This hope is to us the soul's anchor, not cast into the hold of the ship—that is, dependent on our own frames and experiences—nor resting on the shifting sands of human systems of thought; but fastened to the propitiatory, the mercyseat, inside the veil. This anchor has been carried in by Jesus our Forerunner. So that though while here on earth we are tossed about on the sea of time, "our anchor holds within the veil."

It has been pointed out by others that the word translated "forerunner" was a nautical term used to designate a small boat. The mouths of many of the Greek harbors were not passable at low tide by heavy ships on account of the sand bars. It was customary to place the anchor in the forerunner and, rowing over the bar, to cast it in the harbor, thus securing the ship until the tide should rise. The figure is readily applied to the soul's relation to our ascended Lord, who now ministers in the holiest on our behalf, a High Priest according to the order of Melchisedec (20). He has entered into the very presence of God as our representative, and His presence there is the pledge that we will soon follow.

CHAPTER SEVEN

THE SUPERIORITY OF THE MELCHISEDEC PRIESTHOOD

We have seen how in Hebrews 5:5-10 the apostle began to speak of the Melchisedec priesthood of Christ. But from chapter 5:11 to chapter 6:20 he turned aside into a lengthy parenthesis in order to prepare his readers for a better understanding of this important subject. In Hebrews 7 he developed it fully. In the first three verses he concentrated on Melchisedec himself, and incidentally gave a wonderful key to the interpretation of the types found in the Old Testament. He also gave a remarkable confirmation of the doctrine of verbal inspiration.

The Royal Priest (7:1-10)

There is no reason to think of Melchisedec as a mysterious person, possibly supernatural, or even as some have supposed a preincarnate appearance of our Lord Jesus Christ. If any ask, "Who is Melchisedec?" the only proper answer is "Melchisedec." He was not Shem the son of Noah, nor Job of the land of Uz, nor Cheops the builder of the great pyramid, as some have endeavored to prove. He was, as is distinctly stated, Melchisedec, King of Salem. All that we know of him is given us in Genesis 14:18-20. This historical account depicted him as a royal priest reigning in Salem, the city that was afterwards known as Jerusalem. Long before the Levitical economy had been established and a special family set apart for the priesthood he, like Job and Abraham, offered sacrifices as a priest of the Most High God. In the divine providence he met Abraham and his triumphant band as they returned from defeating Chedorlaomer and his allies. It is noticeable that the King of Sodom was on his way to meet Abraham when the latter was intercepted by Melchisedec, who came to bless him in the name of the Most High God. Abraham recognized Melchisedec's spiritual authority by giving him tithes of all the spoils. Strengthened by the bread and wine administered by Salem's king-priest, Abraham was prepared to refuse the blandishments of the King of Sodom, representative of the world in all its impurity and debasement.

In Psalm 110 our Lord is prophetically saluted as a Priest forever after the order of Melchisedec. Christ is to come forth from the new Jerusalem after the Armageddon conflict as a royal Priest to bless His delivered people in that day of His power.

Now observe how remarkably the Spirit of God sets His seal on the verbal inspiration of the Old Testament. Our attention is drawn to the fact that this royal hierarch is first "by interpretation King of righteousness, and after that also King of Salem, which is, King of peace" (Hebrews 7:2). If the order of the names had been reversed, God's beautiful type would have been spoiled. But standing just as they do, the names *righteousness* and *Salem* are in perfect agreement with truth revealed elsewhere. Righteousness must come before peace. We are told in Isaiah 32:17, "The work of righteousness shall be peace; and the effect of righteousness quietness and assurance forever." And in the great gospel Epistle to the Romans we first learn how the righteousness of God has been maintained in the cross before we are told of peace with God, which is ours by faith. So exact is Scripture that the changing of the order of the original words would throw all into confusion.

Hebrews 7:3 has perplexed many, but it simply declares that so far as Scripture is concerned, Melchisedec appears on its sacred page "without father, without mother, without descent [or genealogy], having neither beginning of days, nor end of life; but made like unto the Son of God; abideth a priest continually." That is, in the book of Genesis, in which we find so many genealogies, Melchisedec, in spite of his importance, has none. There is no record of his parentage, his birth, or his death. He simply appears for a moment, then vanishes from our sight, never even to be mentioned again in the Word of God until the prophecy of Psalm 110. Thus he is an apt type of our ever-living Savior and High Priest. Again let us worship as we contemplate the perfection of Scripture—just as perfect in what it omits as in what it relates!

In Hebrews 7:4-10 we have the superiority of the Melchisedec priesthood over that of Levi brought out very clearly. Levi was not born until many years after the event mentioned in Genesis 14. Abraham, however, was the father of all the Hebrew race. Therefore all the twelve tribes, including Levi from whom came the priestly family, were represented in Abraham when he recognized the superiority of Melchisedec by paying tithes to him and received his high priestly blessing. Unquestionably, wrote the apostle, "the less is blessed of the better;" and so in this double way the surpassing greatness of this royal priest is emphasized. "Levi," we are told, "who receiveth tithes, paid tithes in Abraham. For he was yet in the loins of his father, when Melchisedec met him" (9-10). Just as the entire human race was on trial in Adam, so the Levitical priesthood was represented in the patriarch Abraham when he acknowledged the superiority of Melchisedec by his attitude toward him.

Jesus Like Melchisedec (7:11-28)

The ground is now clear to show how the Melchisedec priesthood of our Lord Jesus Christ surpasses in every way the Aaronic. It is evident that if perfection had come under the Levitical priesthood, in connection with which the law was given, there would have been no occasion for God to set it aside and raise up another priest after a different and better order. Our Lord's priesthood was after the character of Aaron; that is, His Person and work were typified by the high priest and his service in connection with the tabernacle. But He does not belong to that order. He is, as was Melchisedec, King and Priest by divine fiat, not by human succession. This involved a complete setting aside of the old covenant, for "the priesthood being changed, there is made of necessity a change also of the law" (12). Israel stood or fell with the priesthood. If God accepted the high priest on the great day of atonement, for instance,

it involved the acceptance of the nation. If the high priest was rejected, then the people were set aside. No high priest was ever to
rend his garments (Leviticus 10:6). When Caiaphas in his excite-
ment and indignation tore his clothes, the priesthood passed away
from the house of Aaron (Matthew 26:65). And with it went the
entire legal economy, which was superseded by the marvelous dispensation of the grace of God.

According to Levitical law, our Lord had no title to the priesthood at all. As to His lineage, He came from the tribe of Judah, not
from that of Levi; but this does not in any way militate against His
priesthood since it is of an altogether different order (Hebrews 7:14).
He is consecrated, not in accordance with a legal enactment, but in
all the might of resurrection "after the power of an endless life"
(16).

As Priest forever after the order of Melchisedec, He has brought
in a new and better regime than that of the law (17-18). And so the
commandment going before has been set aside. It was weak and
unprofitable in the sense that it could not accomplish that for which
it was proposed—namely, to give man a righteous standing before
God. The law failed because the flesh or the carnal mind "is not
subject to the law of God, neither indeed can be" (Romans 8:7). So
it was useless as a ground for blessing. It made nothing perfect;
therefore it had to give way to the introduction of a better hope by
which we draw near to God (Hebrews 7:19). This better hope is
founded upon the principle of grace of which Melchisedec is the
exemplification. And so by divine oath Jesus has become the guar-
antee of a better covenant.

In Hebrews 7:23-28 the contrast is between the dying priests of
the old order and the ever living High Priest at God's right hand.
There was a constant succession of priests in olden days, for death
was continually taking its toll of them. But our Lord's priesthood is
unchangeable because He continues "unto the ages," the strongest
expression in the Greek language for eternity.

Thus He is able to deliver completely those who draw near to
God by Him, seeing He lives forever to make intercession for them.
It should be noted that salvation "to the uttermost" (25) does not
simply mean salvation from every kind of sin, but is even greater

than that—salvation forevermore. He whom God saves is saved eternally, for Christ who died for him now lives to keep him and to
complete the work He began. And thus our souls are stirred to worship and thanksgiving as we realize how suited our Great High Priest
is to the need of those who were once unholy, harmful and defiled,
sinful and degraded. He gives us a perfect representation before the
throne of God. He is everything that we were not and should have
been. He is holy, harmless, undefiled, and separate from sinners
and higher than the heavens, and He is all this for us (26).

Nor is it necessary that He, like the high priests of old, should
offer daily sacrifices (27). They offered for their own sins, for they
were themselves unclean, and then they offered in behalf of the
people. But these sacrifices never settled the sin question. Christ,
by His one offering up of Himself upon the cross, has completed
the work that saves, and settled the sin question for all eternity. The
law constituted men high priests who were themselves infirm and
unreliable, but the divine oath has proclaimed Jesus to be a Priest
forever, He who is the Son of the eternal Father.

What could the Spirit of God Himself say to make clearer the
superiority of the priesthood of the new dispensation over that of
the old? And with the priesthood, of course, is linked the entire
sacrificial system. No Jew ever found settled peace or a purged conscience through recourse to the altar and the priest of the tabernacle
or the temple. Undoubtedly wherever there was real faith, God met
His people in grace. Through the Spirit He gave them an inward
sense of acceptance and joy in Himself, but this was not based on
the Levitical system. It was all in view of the eventual coming into
the world of the Seed of the woman, who was to bruise the serpent's
head. He Himself would be wounded for His people's transgressions and bruised for their iniquities. The pious Israelite obeyed the
commandment of the law and acted in accordance with the Mosaic
ritual because God had ordained that system for that time. Faith
would lead him to do exactly as the Lord had said, but the ground of
his peace rested not on the typical system but on that which it illustrated, the finished work of Christ. It was hard even for converted
Hebrews to fully understand this concept. Therefore we see the care
with which the Holy Spirit through the apostle described each

detail in His effort to deliver them from Judaism and bring them out into the full light and liberty of Christianity.

In closing our study of this chapter, I would point out the distinction between the expression used in Hebrews 7:27, "he offered up himself," and that found in 9:14 where we read, "Christ, who through the eternal Spirit offered himself without spot to God." He "offered himself" at His baptism in the Jordan, when the Holy Spirit descended upon Him. The Spirit revealed the Father's good pleasure and pointed to Christ as the perfect sacrifice, who alone was able to fulfill all righteousness on behalf of guilty sinners. But it was at the cross that He actually "offered up himself" and voluntarily became the great sin offering. It is important to remember that the death of Jesus was not merely man's answer to the grace of God as seen in Christ. None could have put Him to death had He not of His own volition yielded up His life. He Himself declared, "No man taketh [my life] from me, but I lay it down of myself. I have power to lay it down, and I have power to take it again. This commandment have I received of my Father" (John 10:18). In the fullest possible sense He laid down that life voluntarily when He allowed wicked men to nail Him to that cross. There He took the sinner's place and bore the sinner's judgment. We speak of this as the finished work of Christ. But when we think of His high priesthood we are on other ground altogether. This is His unfinished work, the work that will never be completed as long as any of His redeemed are in the place of testing and in need of help.

CHAPTER EIGHT

THE MEDIATOR OF THE NEW COVENANT

In Hebrews 8 we are given a summary of the instruction we have already received concerning the priesthood of our blessed Lord.

The Ascended Priest (8:1-6)

We see in Christ a High Priest who through His own inherent right has taken a place that no Levitical priest could ever take. The high priest of the old covenant was merely permitted to enter once a year into the holy of holies, and that only for a few moments, not daring to sit down in the presence of God. However our Lord Jesus Christ, as the ascended man, has entered into the heavenly sanctuary and is there seated on the right hand of the throne of the Majesty. There He ministers in the holiest in that glorious tabernacle of which the earthly tent was but a type.

How important it is for us to realize that we are represented before God by a man in the glory. For though we no longer know Christ in the flesh, yet He has gone up to Heaven as the representative man to appear in the presence of God on our behalf.

The earthly high priest of old was appointed to offer both gifts and sacrifices (3). By gifts we understand those offerings that were the expression of the grateful, adoring hearts of the people of Israel. The sacrifices, on the other hand, had to do directly with making expiation for sin. Our Lord did this latter when He offered Himself up on the cross. But now that He is ministering in the heavenly sanctuary, it is of course necessary that He have something to offer. He presents our prayers and praises before God. Our heartfelt worship ascends to the Father through Him.

> Our great High Priest is sitting
> At God's right hand above;
> For us His hands uplifted
> In sympathy and love.
>
> To all our prayers and praises,
> Christ adds His sweet perfume,
> And love the censer raises,
> These odors to consume.

We may often be discouraged as we realize the imperfections of even our highest and best efforts to glorify God. Like Cowper, we may exclaim: "Sin twines itself about my thoughts, / And slides into my prayers." But it is blessed to know that nothing reaches God that is not perfect. Our Great High Priest takes out of our prayers and praises everything that is unholy or of the flesh, everything that is contrary to the nature of the God we adore. Then to what is left, He adds his own infinite perfections and thus presents all to the Father on our behalf.

His priesthood is altogether heavenly in character, for "if he were on earth, he should not be a priest, seeing that there are priests that offer gifts according to the law: Who serve unto the example and shadow of heavenly things" (4-5). This is not to say that He never acted in a priestly capacity while in this world. He certainly did. As a Priest, He prayed for His disciples. In John 17 we have a wonderful sample of His high priestly intercession. As Priest too, He offered Himself on the cross as the supreme sacrifice for sin, as in the case of Aaron offering the bullock and the goat on the great day of atonement. But the point is, His entire priesthood was heavenly in character. It was not inherited after the Aaronic order. Looked at from that standpoint, He would not be a Priest at all, as He did not belong to the tribe of Levi or the household of Aaron. He is the second man, the Lord from Heaven, and as such He is our Great High Priest, fulfilling the types and shadows of heavenly things, as described, for instance, in the book of Leviticus. In fact everything in connection with the tabernacle and its service was symbolic of Christ, picturing His glorious person and His wondrous work. This was why God was so particular in regard to all its details. "Moses was admonished of God," we are told, "when he was about to make the tabernacle: for, See, saith he, that thou make all things according to the pattern shewed to thee in the mount" (Hebrews 8:5). There was no room for human ingenuity or for Moses' own thoughts. All must be as ordered by God, for He alone knew the Son and the work He was to accomplish.

Now that the symbolic dispensation has been replaced by the present economy of grace, Christ has entered upon His better ministry, because He is the Mediator of a better covenant that was established upon better promises (6). The old covenant depended on man's ability to carry out its requirements. God in effect said, "If you will do thus and so, I will do certain things." Thus the promise of blessing rested on man's ability to claim that blessing on the ground of his obedience to the law. No man ever could obtain the promises on that basis. And so our Lord Jesus took upon Himself the curse of a broken law, was made a curse for us, became the great sin offering, and now has become the Mediator of a better covenant. In this covenant all the promise is on God's part and man receives every blessing as pure grace.

The Better Covenant (8:7-13)

Had that first covenant been perfect, it would never have been set to one side and a new covenant brought in. But because of its imperfection on account of the weakness and frailty of the flesh, God had declared long before the coming of our Lord Jesus Christ into the world that a new covenant was to be consummated with Israel and Judah. In verses 8-12 the apostle quoted from Jeremiah

31:31-34. The new covenant is clearly a reaffirmation of the unconditional covenant made with Abraham. The law, which came in centuries later, could not annul the covenant with Abraham. During all
the present years of wandering, Israel and Judah are under the curse
of that broken law. But in the regeneration, when they will be gath-
ered back to their own land and restored to the favor of the Lord,
this covenant of grace will be made with them.

It is most important to realize that nowhere are we told of a covenant made with the church. In Romans 9:4 we learn that "the
covenants" pertained to Israel. They were the chosen people with
whom the Sinaitic covenant was made. According to the terms of
that covenant they have forfeited all claim on God's favor. But He
cannot deny Himself. He can never go back on the covenant made
with Abraham, by the terms of which He promised blessing uncon-
ditionally to Abraham's seed. He reiterated these promises in the
new covenant. The blood of that covenant has been shed on the
cross. Our Lord said, as He gave the communion cup to His disciples, "This is the new covenant in my blood which is shed for
you." On the basis of that precious blood all who now believe in
Him who shed it, enter into the spiritual blessings of the new covenant, even though Gentiles after the flesh, and therefore by nature.
"strangers from the covenants of promise" (Ephesians 2:12). But in
the fullness of times, when the day of Israel's blessing will arrive,
the new covenant will be confirmed to them and they will be born
of God—"a nation shall be born in a day"—and He will own them
as His covenant people. His laws will then be instilled in their minds
and written upon their hearts. They will render to Him glad, happy
service, not in order to make themselves worthy of covenant blessing, but because of the gladness of their souls when they know Him
as their God and realize that they are indeed His ransomed people.
The day of their blindness will have gone forever. The veil will be
taken away from their hearts. No longer in need of human instruction, they will all know the Lord from the least to the greatest. In
that wondrous day He will be merciful to their unrighteousness and
will remember their sins and iniquities no more.

While this does not reach the full height of Christian blessing, yet it will be wonderful grace indeed shown to the people who failed so terribly when they crucified the Lord of glory. The new covenant says nothing of entrance into the holiest, as we now know it; nothing of being raised up together and seated together in Christ Jesus in the heavenlies; nothing of union with Him as members of His body by the indwelling Holy Spirit. It is blessing for the earth and on the earth in the coming day. But all these heavenly privileges are secured for the church now by the shedding of the same blood of the covenant that is to procure future blessing for Israel. This fact led the apostle in the chapters that follow to stress our present privilege to enter into the holiest, while Israel and Judah are still dispersed among the Gentiles, waiting for the day when the new covenant will be confirmed to them.

The very expression "a new covenant," in itself makes the former testament null and void (13). It served its purpose up to the cross. Now that "which decayeth and waxeth old is ready to vanish away." It is pathetic how few Christians understand that the sacrifice of our Lord Jesus Christ has freed us from all obligation to that temporary dispensation. It is to be feared that many who sometimes sing of such liberty fail really to understand its import.

> Free from the law! Oh, happy condition!
> Jesus hath bled, and there is remission;
> Cursed by the law and bruised by the fall,
> Christ hath redeemed us once for all.

Many who in a vague way have trusted in Christ and are undoubtedly regenerated, are still far from enjoying the liberty that is ours in Christ. Our present relationship to God is one of pure grace during this parenthetical period. God, having set aside Israel after the flesh, is at this time taking out from among the Gentiles a people for His name. After this work is completed, He will build again the tabernacle of David that is fallen down. He will make a new covenant with those in Israel and Judah who turn to the Lord in that day.

The important thing to see is that the new covenant, as such, does not go beyond blessing on the earth. It has to do with the earthly side of the kingdom of God. The new birth is a prerequisite to membership in that kingdom, as our Lord told Nicodemus. This is what is meant by the writing of the divine law upon the hearts in the day that Israel and Judah will turn to the One who was once rejected.

CHAPTER NINE
THE PERFECTION OF CHRIST'S WORK

(PART ONE)

As we enter now into the very heart of this precious portion of God's Word, the apostle at the outset directs our attention to the typical character of the sanctuary and its service under the former dispensation. Note that throughout this chapter he has the tabernacle in view rather than the temple. This is not, as some have supposed, because the construction of the temple was any less divinely ordered than that of the tabernacle. David plainly declared to Solomon, in giving him the plan for the more permanent sanctuary, "All this...the Lord made me understand in writing by his hand upon me, even all the works of this pattern" (1 Chronicles 28:19). But the temple symbols evidently prefigure millennial glory and blessing and will be fully revealed and understood in that day of Jehovah's power. The tabernacle, on the other hand, which was a temporary dwelling place picturing truth for a pilgrim people, has its application to the present times. For the Holy Spirit, typified by the cloudy pillar, is now leading the new dispensation company through the wilderness of this world, on to the rest that remains for the people of God.

The Earthly Sanctuary a Shadow of the Heavenly (9:1-10)

As the first covenant was for a limited time, so with the first tabernacle. It had ordinances of divine service and a worldly sanctuary. By "worldly" we are not to understand "unspiritual," but rather that which is in contrast with the heavenly.

The tabernacle itself was divided into two parts, the first called the holy place, and the second, the holiest of all, separated by the sacred veil. And as the apostle pointed out the various pieces of furniture connected with each, we have another most striking illustration of the absolute verbal inspiration of the Holy Scriptures.

When he wrote of the first compartment, he said, "Wherein was the candlestick and the table, and the shewbread" (2). He made no mention of the golden altar of incense. Had he forgotten that this altar stood immediately before the veil? Or was there some divine reason for omitting mention of it in this connection? Unbelievers have eagerly seized upon this, claiming that it showed the inaccuracy on the part of the sacred writer.

However all becomes very clear when we carefully note the next three verses:

> And after the second veil, the tabernacle which is called the Holiest of all; Which had the golden censer, and the ark of the covenant overlaid round about with gold, wherein was the golden pot that had manna, and Aaron's rod that budded, and the tables of the covenant; And over it the cherubims of glory shadowing the mercyseat; of which we cannot now speak particularly (3-5).

Observe carefully the change from the expression "wherein" (2) to the altogether different term "which had" (4). And then notice that the golden censer is really the golden incense altar. The original is *thumiasterion*, which is the ordinary word for an incense altar. It is not at all the same as the word *libanotos* used in Revelation 8:3,5 for a censer. Any ordinary reader of English can see how utterly different the two words are. There can be no question, then, but that *censer* in Hebrews 9:4 means the incense altar. But why did the writer not say it was in the holy place? Why does he plainly connect it with the holiest? The answer is perfectly simple. It belonged to the holiest because it typified Christ's person and intercessory work in the holiest of all. But during all the Old Testament dispensation it must stand outside the veil where it could be approached by the priests. Yet it stood so near the veil that the moment this curtain was torn in two from the top to the bottom, the fragrant smoke of the incense entered the holiest. The apostle does not say it was in the holiest, but he does declare it belonged to the holiest "which had the golden incense [altar]." So then the apparent imperfection is really a most beautiful evidence of the perfection of Holy Writ.

As long as the old dispensation lasted the priests had no access into the holiest. They went only into the first tabernacle and accomplished the liturgical service. Once a year the high priest alone was permitted to enter the sacred inner chamber where the shekinah hovered over the mercyseat. Nor could he approach without atoning blood, which he offered first of all for himself as being but a sinful man, and also for the failures of the people (7).

By this arrangement, the Holy Spirit was declaring the solemn fact that the way into the immediate presence of God had not yet been made known, nor could be, so long as that first tabernacle had any standing before Him. The expression "was yet standing" is misleading (8). It would suggest that the way into the holiest was not made known until the destruction of the temple about A.D. 70, and thus many have understood it. But it clearly means that the way into the holiest was not opened up so long as God recognized the first tabernacle. The moment Christ Jesus died on the cross the entire typical system ceased to have any standing before God. It was but a figure for a time, and the gifts and sacrifices offered in connection with it were simply picturing the offering up of the body of our Lord Jesus Christ upon the cross. In themselves, the sacrifices were of no real value. They could not settle the sin question, and therefore could not perfect the consciences of those who brought them (9). The many ordinances in connection with meats and drinks and different baptisms, whether of persons or things, in fact all the fleshly observances that were connected with the first covenant, were only intended to serve a temporary purpose. These regulations were only in force until the time of reformation—that is, until Christ by His death and resurrection fulfilled them all and brought in the present new and glorious dispensation of the grace of God.

The Superior Sacrifice of Christ (9:11-23)

The apostle now proceeds to show how marvelously the one offering of our Lord Jesus Christ transcends all the types and shadows of the old covenant. He is both High Priest and victim. As High Priest of good things to come He has by the presentation of His blood entered in once for all into the holiest on the basis of an accomplished redemption. His ministry is linked with a greater and more perfect tabernacle—that is, with the eternal dwelling place of God (11). His work abides eternally before God. No failure on the part of His redeemed can touch the value of His finished work. Under the old covenant, every time an Israelite sinned he needed a new sacrifice; but Christ's one perfect offering up of Himself has settled the sin question forever. Therefore no wandering of heart or failure in life by those who by faith have availed themselves of His atoning work can alter for one moment their standing before the throne of God.

> That which can shake the cross
> Can shake the peace it gave;
> Which tells me Christ has never died,
> Nor ever left the grave.

Because of the infinite value of His precious blood, He has fully met all the claims of divine justice and thus secured eternal redemption. The moment His blood was shed on the cross its efficacy was recognized in Heaven, thus fulfilling the sprinkling of the blood on the mercyseat. But it is not only seen as sprinkled on the throne of God but also on the believer, who is thus purged from all uncleanness.

Verse 13 brings vividly before us the ordinance of the red heifer as given in Numbers 19. The heifer was burned to ashes, the ashes mixed with water, and this water of separation was sprinkled upon an unclean Israelite in order to make him fit for participation in the service of the earthly sanctuary. Ashes in this connection became eloquent indeed. They cried aloud, as did our dying Savior, "It is finished"! For ashes tell of fire burned out never to burn again. And so the failing believer has daily recourse to the washing of water by the Word, bringing afresh to his soul the truth of that finished work wherein every sin was settled. Therefore the apostle said, "How much more shall the blood of Christ, who through the eternal Spirit offered himself without spot to God, purge your conscience from dead works to serve the living God?" (Hebrews 9:14) He, the sinless One, offered Himself to take the sinner's place, and this in the power of the eternal Spirit. Through the shedding of His blood our consciences are cleansed from works of death and we are set free to serve the living God. The Israelite under the old covenant who was defiled by coming in contact with the dead, had recourse to the water of separation. But all our best efforts were defiled by the fact that we ourselves in our unsaved state were dead in trespasses and sins. Now, with all the past settled for, we are free to serve the living God in faith and in the power of a new life.

Christ is therefore the Mediator of the new covenant, which is founded on His own death. By His death He settled for the sins of all who turned to God in faith during the times of the first covenant, that they, with us, might receive the promise of the eternal inheritance. This is undoubtedly the meaning of the expression, "the redemption of the transgressions that were under the first testament" (15). The sins of Old Testament saints were not actually put away until Christ accomplished redemption on the cross. Then these believers came into all the blessing of the new covenant, which He sealed with His own blood.

The old covenant was God's will for His people prior to the coming of Christ. It was sealed by the blood of calves and goats, which Moses sprinkled on the book and all the people saying, "This is the blood of the testament which God hath enjoined unto you" (19-20). The new covenant is the will of our blessed Lord whereby He decrees that all who put their trust in Him should receive part in that eternal inheritance, which He gladly shares with all believers. By His death this testament came into force. Apart from His death, there could be no such blessing for guilty sinners. A testament is in effect after men are dead. Christ's death on the cross put this new covenant, or testament, or will, into operation. Inasmuch as it is a covenant of pure grace, all who believe experience the good of it even before the day when it is to be openly confirmed with Israel and Judah, as we saw in the previous chapter. The blood of the covenant having already been shed, there is nothing to hinder the flow of blessing. The sprinkling of the blood under the old dispensation confirmed that covenant, and was a warning to the people that death would result for its violation. At the same time it symbolized the shedding of the blood of the new covenant victim. Therefore we are told that Moses sprinkled with blood both the tabernacle and all the vessels of the ministry (21). "Almost all things are by the law purged with blood; and without shedding of blood is no remission" (22). This last statement is absolute. It is not restricted to the old covenant, as the verses that immediately follow make plain.

It was necessary in the plan of God that the patterns and figures of things in the heavens should be purified with the blood of animal sacrifices, but the realities with better sacrifices than those of old. The heavenly things need purification because sin began in the heavens. It was there that Satan fell, and thus the heavens became unclean. Christ's sacrifice is the basis for the purification of the polluted heavens and guarantees the bringing in of a new heaven and a new earth wherein dwelleth righteousness. Thus eventually, all in Heaven and all on earth will be reconciled to God through the blood of the cross.

This, of course, is not universalism. It does not imply the salvation of all who have lived on earth, and certainly not of fallen angels who defiled the heavens. But it does speak of a time coming when sin and sinners will be banished from the earth and the heavens, and God be all in all.

The Way into the Holiest (9:24-28)

Having laid the ground work, the apostle proceeded to open up the special truth of the new dispensation, and to show how fully Christ has superseded all the types of the old covenant. In Hebrews

9:24-28 we have what someone has very aptly designated, the three appearings of our Lord Jesus Christ: He hath appeared, He doth appear, He shall appear. The order, however, is somewhat different, for the Holy Spirit dwells first on His present appearance as our intercessor above. He then turns our minds back to the time when He appeared to settle the sin question. And in the closing verses He carries us forward to the glad hour when Christ will appear the second time for our complete and glorious redemption.

In verse 24 then we look by faith into the true tabernacle, which is above—the holy places not made with hands. There we see our blessed risen Lord as He appears in the presence of God on our behalf. He is there to give us a perfect representation before the throne of God and we are accepted in Him. He is also there to make intercession for us in view of human frailty and tendency to err. And as the apostle John wrote, He is there as our Advocate with the Father, to undertake for us when actual failure has come in and broken communion (1 John 2:1). How full and complete is His present service as He officiates for us in the holy places! We often speak, and rightly so, of the finished work of Christ. This refers of course to His vicarious atonement that took place on the cross. But it is just as scriptural to speak of His unfinished work, if we have in mind this special ministry of intercession that He has been carrying on in the holiest ever since He was received up in glory. This work will never be finished so long as one needy saint is in the place of testing here on earth.

His work on the cross can never be repeated. No repetition is required, for He settled the sin question perfectly when He took our place in judgment. And in this we have the great distinction between the legal sacrifices and His one offering of Himself. In the consummation of the ages He appeared to put away sin by His mighty sacrifice. The offerings of old had to be repeated again and again because they did not possess value sufficient to settle the sin question. But His precious blood poured forth for our redemption was of such infinite value that it is sacrilegious even to think of adding to it in any way. Having officiated at the altar, fulfilling the type of the great day of atonement, He has now gone into the sanctuary in the value of His own blood. By and by He will come out to bless His people as did the priest of old.

> And though a while He be
> Hid from the eyes of men,
> His people look to see
> Their Great High Priest again.

Just as truly as men were under sentence of death with judgment beyond it, so Christ took that sentence upon Himself and was once offered to bear the sins of many. And just as certainly He will appear unto them that look for Him the second time. He will return altogether apart from the sin question, unto the complete and final salvation of all His own. Meantime the Holy Spirit has come to bear witness to the efficacy of His propitiatory work, while He Himself continues His ministry in the heavenly sanctuary.

It ought to be clear that the latter part of verse 28 is not intended to teach that only those who have advanced knowledge of prophecy and therefore live in daily expectation of His second coming will be caught up to meet Him at His return. This is not at all what was in the mind of the writer, and is certainly not the teaching of the Holy Spirit elsewhere in Scripture. But just as all Israel could be said to look for the coming forth of the high priest who had sprinkled the mercyseat with the blood of atonement, so all believers look for the coming again of our Lord Jesus. There may not be much understanding as to the mode of His coming, nor in regard to the order of events, but the renewed heart cries, "Come, Lord Jesus."

CHAPTER TEN
THE PERFECTION OF CHRIST'S WORK

(PART TWO)

In the first eighteen verses of chapter 10 the contrast between the sacrifices under the law and Christ's one offering is brought out more clearly than ever. It is important to follow the argument carefully and notice the close reasoning of the apostle as he contrasts the one with the other. He completed the convincing argument by extending an invitation to all believers to enter the holiest "by a new and living way" (19-22).

The All-Sufficient Sacrifice (10:1-22)

The Levitical economy was but a shadow of the coming good things. It was not an exact delineation of these things. It was therefore impossible that the sacrifices offered on Jewish altars yearly to perpetuity could perfect those who presented them so far as their consciences were concerned. For if the bringing of a lamb or a bullock could have settled the sin question, what necessity would there have been to repeat such a sacrifice? The worshipers, if actually once purged, would have been freed from all conscience of sins. Note carefully, the apostle does not say *consciousness* of sins but *conscience* of sins (2). The distinction is most important. Today I may be conscious of sin in thought, word, and deed, but confessing my sins, I look up into the face of my Father with confidence, knowing that for these very sins the blood of Christ has answered. Thus my conscience is freed from condemnation. This could never be under the former order. Every sin called for a new offering, and then on the great day of atonement there was an annual sacrifice for all Israel.

Notice verse 3: "In those sacrifices there is a remembrance again made of sins every year." Other translations have been suggested, all of which help to throw light on the meaning of this verse. The word translated "remembrance" might be rendered "recognition," "calling to mind," or "acknowledgment." But why such an acknowledgment of sins if the sacrifice could not actually purge them away? The illustration of a promissory note might help here. Let us suppose one is in debt for a certain sum of money. He gives a note to run for a year. At the end of the year he finds himself unable to pay. He renews the note. The note has no real value in itself. In the same way the sacrifices had no moral or spiritual value in the sight of God. But in that note there is an acknowledgment of the debt from year to year. Now let us suppose someone who is well able to pay, endorses the note, what then? When it becomes due, it is referred to him for settlement and he discharges the obligation.

The application is simple and clear. It was not possible that the blood of bulls and of goats should take away sins. But every time a believing Israelite brought his sacrifice to the altar he was, so to speak, giving his note to God. He acknowledged his indebtedness, his sin, and accepted responsibility for the same. This was all he could do, but the preincarnate Christ endorsed every one of the notes and in the fullness of time came prepared to settle in full for all.

> Wherefore when he cometh into the world, he saith, Sacrifice and offering thou wouldest not, but a body hast thou prepared me: In burnt offerings and sacrifices for sin thou hast had no pleasure. Then said I, Lo, I come (in the volume of the book it is written of me), to do thy will, O God (5-7).

Here indeed is the divine endorser who undertakes in grace to meet every claim that the throne of God has against penitent sinners. In this passage, which is quoted from Psalm 40:6-8, it is interesting to observe that all four of the offerings of Leviticus 1 to 7 are in view. The word *sacrifice* refers to the peace offering. The term *offering* is really the *minchah*—that is, the meal offering. The other two terms are too clearly designated to need any explanation. All of these offerings were of no avail to put away sin, and consequently it could be said of them that God had no pleasure in them. But when His own blessed Son came into the world to fulfill all these types, and to pay in His own person the redemption price, it is written: "It pleased the Lord to bruise him; he hath put him to grief: when thou shalt make his soul an offering for sin, he shall see his seed, he shall prolong his days, and the pleasure of the Lord shall prosper in his hand" (Isaiah 53:10).

By the fulfillment of the declaration of Psalm 40 He actually wound up the old dispensation and brought in the new. "He taketh away the first, that he may establish the second" (Hebrews 10:9).

When He said, "I come to do thy will," He spoke of course of the will of God in His coming to make expiation for iniquity. By His accomplishment of that will, we who believe in Him are now eternally set apart to God on the basis, not of our promises or feelings or of our personal righteousness, but of the offering of the body of Jesus Christ once for all. How slowly truths like these seem to seep into our souls and become part of our very beings. But one may safely say there is no lasting peace until this aspect of Christ's work has been laid hold of in faith.

Continuing, the writer reminded his readers that in the sanctuary of old the high priests were constantly ministering and carrying on a work which was never completed, because of the fact that those offerings could not take away sins (11). The expression "every priest standeth" is in itself significant. We do not read of a chair or a settee in the tabernacle or temple, for the priest's work was never done. But how different it is with our Great High Priest above! He, after having offered His one sacrifice for sins forever, sat down on the right hand of God, where He now waits until His enemies be made the footstool of His feet (12-13). Whether one connects the term "forever" with the expression "one sacrifice for sins" or with the sitting down, makes little difference. That sacrifice has eternal efficacy. On the other hand, as priest-victim, His work done, He sat down never to offer sacrifice again. His one offering is perfect and complete, and all who are linked with Him by faith appear before God in all the value of that finished work, perfected forever, because sanctified in Him.

The Holy Spirit testifies of the complete sufficiency of Christ's work (15). He has come forth from the Father and the Son to bear testimony to the perfection of that finished work. And it is He who now opens up the Holy Scriptures of the Old Testament, allowing us to see in them what saints of old never realized was there. Witness the quotation from Jeremiah 31:33-34. What was promised to Israel and Judah through the new covenant is now true of all who turn to Christ. Through the new birth God puts His laws in their hearts and writes them in their minds, and declares without any qualification, "Their sins and iniquities will I remember no more." This is complete justification from all things. No charge can now be brought against the one for whom Christ has settled everything. Therefore the blessed conclusion, "Where remission of these is, there is no more offering for sin" (Hebrews 10:18).

This complete forgiveness entitles the "brethren" of Christ, the new priestly house, to enter with boldness as purged worshipers into the holiest, the immediate presence of God. They enter in all the infinite value of the blood of Jesus through that new and living way, which He Himself opened for us. By His death on the cross the veil was torn in two and God no longer was hidden, and man in Christ was no longer shut out. So intimately are the redeemed and the Redeemer linked together, so truly are the High Priest and priestly house one before God, that we are urged to enter in spirit where He has gone. We are exhorted to draw near to God with true hearts in the full assurance of that faith that is based on the knowledge of an accomplished redemption. For our hearts have been sprinkled by the blood of Christ from an evil conscience, and like the once-defiled Israelite, "our bodies [have been] washed with pure water."

It is to be regretted that so few Christians seem to apprehend all this today. It is safe to say that for thousands who have hope in Christ, the veil might just as well never have been torn. They do not have any conception of liberty for access into the holiest, but think of themselves as a people still on probation. They think that if only they are faithful to their profession they will eventually be fitted for admission into the presence of God. How much is lost through failure to understand the true Christian position, which has been beautifully expressed in the words of an old hymn:

> Now we see in Christ's acceptance,
> But the measure of our own;
> He who lay beneath our sentence
> Seated high upon the throne.

God sees every believer in Christ, and the feeblest saint has immediate access into the holiest through the atoning blood. The exhortation and warning that follow were never intended by the Holy Spirit to becloud this blessed truth in the slightest degree, but rather to accentuate the importance of holding fast what is here revealed.

Warning Against Apostasy (10:23-39)

After the gracious invitation to enter into the holiest comes the counter exhortation of verses 23-25. In verse 23 *confession* would be a better word than *profession* as in the King James version. We may profess what is not true. We confess that which is. The believer has declared his faith in a crucified, risen, and glorified Christ. He is exhorted to hold fast this great confession without turning either to the right or to the left. The Christian is assured of the faithfulness of Him who gave the promises concerning His Son, and has in grace fulfilled them up to the present moment. One great promise remains to be confirmed at our Lord's return. We may be assured that He who has never failed in one respect in regard to the past and present work of Christ, will be equally faithful in regard to the future.

Three times in this chapter, we have the persuasive words, *let us*. First, "Let us draw near" (22); second, "Let us hold fast" (23); and third, "Let us consider one another" (24). The believer is not alone in his confession of Christ, nor is he to act in isolation. He is linked with others both by nature and grace, and he is called to stir up his brethren to love and good works, assembling with fellow-saints for worship, prayer, and testimony, not coldly withdrawing himself as the manner of some. The believer is exhorted to remember that his responsibility toward his brethren is all the greater if some seem to have failed grievously and others are in danger of failing. He is not to make special light on prophetic truth a reason for assuming a sectarian attitude toward his brethren. He needs them and they need him all the more as the day of Christ's glorious return to this earth approaches.

In verses 26-31 we have another side of things altogether. The warning, as in Hebrews 6, is against apostasy.

The warning is based on the perfection of the one sacrifice of Christ, which had been explained in such a marvelous way in the first 22 verses of Hebrews 10. The warning in chapter 6 was based on the revealed power of the Holy Spirit working in the Christian company, which was designed of God to exalt the person of Christ. To apostatize either from the truth as to His person or His finished work, means eternal ruin. It is not mere failure in the life that is contemplated in Hebrews 10:26. The willful sin in this passage is the definite rejection of His atoning sacrifice. Nor is this simply the foolish and wicked determination of a moment, of which many have been guilty but have afterwards been brought to sincere repentance. The apostle really wrote, "If we are sinning willfully after that we have received the knowledge of the truth, there remains no other sacrifice for sins." The verb is the present participle. It is what has become habitual. If after fully examining what the Old Testament Scriptures teach concerning Christ and His work and comparing it with the New Testament presentation, thus having obtained the knowledge of the truth, one deliberately and persistently rejects it, God has nothing more to say to him. The one who has rejected the truth has spurned the only means of salvation for Jew or Gentile. An apostate Hebrew might have reasoned within himself that the sacrifices still going on at the temple were all that he needed. Therefore, even though he had professed to be a follower of Christ, he would turn back to the sacrificial system. But this would be a fearful mistake. Those sacrifices no longer availed. Christ's atonement alone met the claims of God in respect to sin. And so the apostate had nothing to look forward to but the certainty of divine judgment and flaming wrath.

In the Old Testament, the despiser of the first covenant died without mercy upon the testimony of two or three witnesses (28). But what was his guilt compared to that of the man who had become acquainted with the gospel message, had at one time been intellectually convinced of the truth, but for selfish reasons had finally turned away from it and gone back to Judaism? To do this was to tread under foot the Son of God and count "the blood of the covenant, wherewith he was sanctified, an unholy thing." Obviously this could never be true of one born of God, for the Holy Spirit abiding within would preserve him from so terrible a step. Yet what is the meaning of the expression, "The blood of the covenant, wherewith he was sanctified" (29)? The answer surely is that sanctification is here positional. All Israel was set apart by the blood of the old covenant at Sinai, and yet any Israelite lacking faith could turn from all the privileges that were his by virtue of that blood. In the same way today the entire professing church is set apart to God on earth in the value of the blood of the new covenant. But this does not preclude the possibility of renouncing this covenant sign and refusing the blessedness that it has purchased. The Holy Spirit delights to magnify Christ and to exalt His work. To refuse His testimony is to scorn the Spirit of grace. This expression, "the Spirit of grace," occurs only here in the New Testament, and is found only once in the Old Testament, and that in Zechariah 12:10.

There is a very interesting suggestion in Hebrews 10:30 in corroboration of the position we have already taken as to the authorship of this Epistle. We read, "We know him that hath said, Vengeance belongeth unto me, I will recompense, saith the Lord. And again, The Lord shall judge his people." These quotations are from Deuteronomy 32:35-36. The second one is an exact quotation from the Hebrew, but the first one is quoted neither from the Hebrew nor the Septuagint. It is the writer's own rendering of the passage, and is exactly the same in the Greek as the quotation in Romans 12:19. We know who the author of Romans was. We may be certain that the same hand penned the Epistle to the Hebrews.

This section of warning closes for the moment with the solemn declaration, "It is a fearful thing to fall into the hands of the living

God" (31). All who reject the testimony He has given concerning His Son must meet Him in judgment; and we read elsewhere, "In thy sight shall no man living be justified" (Psalm 143:2). But "he who has died is justified from sin," as a literal rendering of Romans 6:7 tells us.

Satan has used the passage we have been considering to trouble and perplex honest souls whose sensitive consciences accuse them of failure to walk with God as they should. Such have often been made to fear that they were guilty of the willful sin here contemplated. But it is not the question of what is commonly called "backsliding" that is before us. Any true believer may often be guilty of this; but even when overwhelmed with failure, he clings more tenaciously than ever to the fact that Jesus is the only Savior and His sacrifice the only means of deliverance from sin's judgment. The apostate of this chapter has no such hope or consciousness. He has spurned completely both Christ and the cross. He holds the blood of Jesus in contempt, and hence for him there is nothing but doom ahead.

It is evident that from verse 32 to the end of the chapter the writer desired to assure the hearts of all who have really trusted Christ. He wrote that his words on apostasy do not apply to them, while on the other hand he warned them of the danger of turning their back in the slightest degree on any truth that God had revealed. He recalled to their minds the former days, the days when upon first being awakened by the Holy Spirit and enlightened by the truth, they turned from the world for Christ's sake and were content to suffer for His name. They endured a great fight of afflictions, sometimes suffering personally both by reproach and persecution. At other times they suffered the contempt of their former co-religionists because of fellowship with those who were suffering for Christ's sake (33). They had in this way exhibited their love for the apostle, showing him every consideration possible after his imprisonment. They even took joyfully the spoiling of their goods, knowing on the authority of the Word of God that they had in Heaven a better and enduring treasure (34).

Having begun so well, and up to the present time continued in a life of devoted separation to Christ, he exhorted them so to continue to the end. "Cast not away therefore your confidence, which hath great recompense of reward. For ye have need of patience, that after ye have done the will of God, ye might receive the promise" (35-36). Reward is distinguished from salvation. The latter is altogether by grace, and is ours from the moment we believe in the Lord Jesus Christ. But it is at Christ's return that we shall receive our reward. He said, "Behold, I come quickly; and my reward is with me, to give every man according as his work shall be" (Revelation 22:12). In view of this promise, how needful it is that we endure patiently. We are assured that when we have fulfilled the will of God for us, we shall receive in full the promised blessing at His return.

"For yet a little while, and he that shall come will come, and will not tarry" (Hebrews 10:37). This is a paraphrase of Habakkuk 2:3, which in the Septuagint reads, "For the vision is for a time, and it shall shoot forth at the end, and not in vain: though he should tarry, wait for him; for he will surely come and will not delay." The prophet spoke of Christ Himself. He will fulfill every promise made to His suffering people when He returns in power and glory. And His coming will not be long delayed, though it may seem so sometimes to His waiting people. But we need to remember that "one day is with the Lord as a thousand years, and a thousand years as one day" (2 Peter 3:8), so that barely have two days gone by in God's reckoning since Jesus went away.

In the meantime God has said, "The just shall live by faith: but if any man draw back, my soul shall have no pleasure in him" (Hebrews 10:38). This also is a quotation from Habakkuk 2:4. It is remarkable the way a brief text from an obscure Old Testament writer is used by the Spirit of God to emphasize the great truth that is characteristic of the present age—"The just shall live by faith." We are justified by faith; we are maintained in a righteous life by faith; and by faith we live to God. If any, after making a profession of faith, turn back to the old way of life, they prove that there was no real faith in the soul, and God declares, He hath "no pleasure in them."

But how comforting the words with which the chapter closes. What assurance they are designed to impart to every trusting one.

"But we are not of them who draw back unto perdition; but of them that believe to the saving of the soul." There is an intellectual believing that saves no one. One may accept Christianity as a system one day and give it up the next. But he who truly trusts in Christ is saved even now, and will never draw back unto eternal loss. Concerning these true believers our Lord has said, "Those that thou gavest me I have kept, and none of them is lost" (John 17:12). And we are told that He who hath begun a good work in them will perform it unto the day of Christ (Philippians 1:6). Therefore it should be plain that salvation is not in our keeping, but we ourselves are kept by the power of God. None can pluck us out of the hands of the Father and the Son. Eternal life would not be "eternal" if it were forfeitable and could ever be lost.

CHAPTER ELEVEN

THE PATH OF FAITH

S omeone has called Hebrews 11 God's honor roll. It is indeed a wonderful record of the triumphs of faith on the part of
eminent servants of God in four different dispensations: Abel,
Enoch, and Noah, in antediluvian days; Noah and Abraham in the
dispensation of government; then Abraham after the promise of the
seed, to Joseph the patriarch; and Moses and the other worthies of
the dispensation of law. All these were but preparatory periods leading on to the present glorious dispensation of the grace of God. But
in all these past ages we see that faith was the controlling power
that enabled men to walk with God and triumph over the corrupting
influences of their times.

It is important to remember that God has never had two ways of
saving men. While the revelation of His grace has come gradually,
and various rites and ceremonies have been linked with it at different times, these latter have had nothing to do with regenerating or
justifying the individual. It has always been true that faith in God's
word, whatever that word may have been, has alone justified man
before Him. Through that word men have been saved in all ages,
thus entering into His spiritual kingdom and recognizing His authority in a world at variance with that divine rule. This comes out
very clearly in our present chapter.

The Nature of Faith (11:1-3)

"Faith is the substantiating of things hoped for, the conviction of
things not seen," as another has translated it. That is, faith in what

99

God has declared gives the soul absolute assurance and firm conviction of the reality of things that the natural eye has never seen.
Yet these things are as real to the man of faith as anything that he
can see, feel, taste, smell, or hear. In fact, through faith they become even more real, for his senses might deceive him but the Word
of God he knows to be absolutely infallible. It was this positive
realization that every word of God is true that brought newness of
life to believers in ancient times. Faith enabled them to bear testimony to things that the natural man could never apprehend by such
evidence as appeals to the mind.

Men have speculated all through the centuries as to the origin of
the universe, and have questioned whether matter is eternal or
whether it was directly created by God. But apart from revelation,
no man can speak with certainty in regard to these things. Faith
alone gives apprehension of the truth. By faith we understand that
the worlds were made by the word of God, so that the things which
we now see were brought into existence at His command out of
nothing (3). It is well known that the word translated "worlds" really means "ages," but the last part of the sentence indicates that the
apostle had the material creation in view. But it is the material creation as passing through a series of changing ages, all of which
were planned beforehand by God Himself for the glory of His Son.

What a magnificent conception is this and how far beyond the
highest thoughts of mere natural scientists! Reverent, God-fearing
men of science have always recognized the necessity of this divine
revelation regarding the origin of matter, and have no difficulty with
the sublime narrative of Genesis 1. Unbelief and willful rejection of
the testimony of God makes men stumble at and pervert so wondrous a revelation of the beginnings of the created heavens and earth.
Faith bows in subjection to the witness God has given and glorifies
Him for such a marvelous unfolding of the divine wisdom. The late
F. W. Grant has aptly pointed out the incongruity of the position of
a scientist like Charles Darwin, whose great book, *The Origin of
Species*, was hailed by many as throwing a flood of light on the
method of creation. Yet in that very book, Darwin never touched
the question of origins! In the very nature of things he cannot do so,
for no man who is not subject to the Holy Spirit knows anything

whatever about the beginnings of the material universe and the creatures living in it. But to faith all is plain. The simplest Christian with his Bible before him would say, "Through faith we understand."

Faith Exemplified in Antediluvian Times (11:4-7)

Three men are selected by the Holy Spirit from the dispensation of conscience, which extended from the expulsion of our first parents from Eden to the destruction of the existing world by the flood. Eliphaz, in the book of Job, directs attention to "the old way which wicked men have trodden ... whose foundation was overflown with a flood: Which said unto God, Depart from us" (Job 22:15-17). The author of Hebrews, on the other hand, asked us to contemplate three men who found their delight in God. They glorified Him by faith in a day when corruption and violence were rapidly filling the earth.

In Abel we have the basic truth that approach to God is on the ground of the sacrifice of a living creature whose blood was designed by God to illustrate the sacrifice and death of His own blessed Son. It was not any mere assumption or simply an arbitrary act of his will that led Abel to select a lamb of the flock for his offering. This is evident from the fact that we are told, "By faith Abel offered unto God a more excellent sacrifice than Cain." Faith is taking God at His word. Therefore we are to understand that God Himself had revealed the truth that approach to Him must be by sacrifice. Cain impudently ignored this revelation. Abel acted in accordance with God's revealed will, and in so doing, "obtained testimony that he was righteous, God testifying of his gifts; and by it he being dead yet speaketh" (Hebrews 11:4). His righteousness consisted in believing God and acting accordingly.

In Enoch we see a further truth illustrated. He walked with God by faith, and faith that triumphed over death. He was taken to Heaven without dying. As in the case of Elijah afterwards, men looked in vain for his body. He was not found because God had taken him away. Before his rapture, he had the testimony that he pleased God. We may well be reminded of our Lord's words, "I am the resurrection, and the life: he that believeth in me, though he were dead, yet shall he live: And whosoever liveth and believeth in me shall never die" (John 11:25-26). Just as Enoch was taken away before the judgment of the flood came, so those now who walk by faith and are living on the earth at the return of our Lord Jesus to gather His own to Himself, will be caught up to meet Him in the air without passing through death.

Thus we see that Enoch's faith and ours are of the same character. We see that he was a regenerated man who was justified before God and walked with God in the power of faith. "Without faith it is impossible to please him." The natural man could not in any dispensation live to the glory of God, therefore the need of a second birth. For he that would draw nigh to God must have faith in Him, truly believing that He exists and that He will reward those who seek Him out. This is in full accord with the great declaration of Romans 2:6-8. No man in any dispensation honestly sought after God and failed to find Him, for He always revealed Himself to faith.

In Noah we have faith triumphing over judgment. Again we are called to contemplate a man who in a dark and difficult day heard the voice of God in his inmost soul. God warned Noah concerning something that in the very nature of things, he could not see; but he believed God and, "moved with fear, prepared an ark to the saving of his house." By acting thus upon the word of the Lord, "he condemned the world, and became heir of the righteousness which is by faith." The very building of the ark was in itself a sermon to the antediluvians. Every tap of Noah's hammer was a part of his preaching of righteousness to that generation. It declared him to be a man of faith, and it showed their utter unbelief.

When God said to Noah, "Come thou and all thy house into the ark; for thee have I seen righteous before me in this generation" (Genesis 7:1), He was speaking primarily of the righteousness that is by faith. But where there is real faith in the soul, the life will correspond to that righteousness which is divinely imputed.

Faith in View of the Promised Seed (11:8-16)

Noah belongs to two dispensations. His testimony closed that in which man had been tried and found wanting under conscience. As he stepped out of the ark and built his altar on the new earth, another dispensation began—that of human government, and of promise and testimony—which we generally speak of as the patriarchal age. In this period Abraham became the distinctive figure, though God graciously gives a very large place to the faith of Sara, his wife. The casual reader of the record in Genesis might wonder at her inclusion in this chapter of Hebrews. He may imagine that Sara had very little faith indeed, when she had to be reproved by the angel for her unseemly laughter in the face of the divine declaration that she would have a son.

The very first step that Abraham took, as recorded in the Word, was one of faith. "By faith Abraham, when he was called to go out into a place which he should after receive for an inheritance, obeyed; and he went out, not knowing whither he went" (8). There is no mention here of his failures—the stop in Haran, or the fact that he did not immediately separate himself from his kindred, but that actually his father seems to have taken the initiative in this first step (Genesis 11:31). But the faith that led to the entire movement was that of Abraham, to whom God had revealed Himself in Ur of the Chaldees. According to the statement of Joshua, there can be little doubt that Abraham's family was idolatrous. He said, "Your fathers dwelt on the other side of the flood in old time, even Terah, the father of Abraham, and the father of Nachor: and they served other gods" (Joshua 24:2). But the living God revealed Himself to a young man brought up in these circumstances, and from that moment faith sprang up in Abraham's soul. He was a new man, born of God, though he did not yet have the clear testimony that he was justified by faith. That came later with the fuller revelation of the promised seed.

By faith he traveled the pilgrim path, dwelling as a stranger in the land of promise. His tent and his altar witnessed to the double character of the pilgrim and the worshiper. Isaac and Jacob, the heirs with him of the same promise, followed his example. Hebrews 11:10 suggests that God had made wonderful revelations to Abraham, which are not recorded in the Old Testament, for we read, "He looked for a city which hath foundations, whose builder and maker is God." This city is never described for us until we come to the closing chapters of the book of Revelation. It is the home of all the saints of God, and toward that Abraham looked. Because of its glory, he counted things then present as of little importance.

Sara's faith, though obscured at times, shines out brightly indeed when we remember how utterly impossible from a human stand-point it was that she would ever become the mother of the promised child. That there was a breakdown on the part of both herself and her husband—a breakdown that brought Hagar into the home and led to unhappy circumstances later—is perfectly true, but all this was only temporary. That which God delights to remember of Sara is that she counted Him faithful who promised. And so the apostle reminded us, "Therefore sprang there even of one, and him as good as dead, so many as the stars of the sky in multitude, and as the sand which is by the sea shore innumerable" (12).

So this particular section concludes with the declaration that all of these died in faith. They left this world without having received all that was promised, but the promises became to them very real. They laid hold of these promises, and because of them confessed themselves strangers and pilgrims on the earth. To relinquish present things in view of future blessing is to declare openly that one is seeking a country. No one can truly relinquish this world below until he has seen by faith a better and brighter world above. Had the patriarchs desired, they could have returned to the temporal things from which God had called them, but they sought a better—that is, a heavenly country. They let go of present advantage as they reached out for that which God had promised. Therefore, it is His delight to acknowledge them now as His own, and to link His name with theirs for whom He has prepared a city. May it be ours to follow in their train, and thus as strangers and pilgrims press on to the rest that remains for the people of God. One is reminded of J. Denham Smith's beautiful words:

> Rise up and hasten
> My soul, haste along!
> And speed on thy journey
> With hope and with song.
> Home, home is nearing
> 'Tis coming into view,

A little more of toiling,
And then to earth adieu.

Why should we linger
When Heaven lies before?
Earth's fast receding,
And soon will be no more;
Its joys and its treasures,
Which once here we knew,
Now never more can charm us,
With such a goal in view.

Faith Exemplified in the Patriarchs (11:17-22)

Beginning with the seventeenth verse we have another distinct series of people bearing witness to the power of faith. Abraham is brought in again, but in an altogether different connection. Heretofore he has been before us as the expectant believer waiting on God to fulfill His promise to give him a son. We have seen how that faith was rewarded in due time, after nature had been proved to be completely powerless and as good as dead. Now we have the same patriarch manifesting faith under new and even more trying circumstances. The promised son had been given, but to the father's heart there came the demand from God to give that son back to Him. This was to be done in such a way as to prefigure the sacrifice of God's own Son on the cross, and in a manner that transcended every other Old Testament type. The scene in Genesis 22 is one that moves every regenerated soul to worship and praise as he reads it. There we read of the father and the son going to the place of sacrifice. Twice in that chapter we get the tender and meaningful words, "They went both of them together" (6,8). How strikingly this phrase illustrates that mystic journey of the Father and the Son from the throne of glory to the cross of Calvary. Of these divine persons it may also be said, "They went both of them together." It tells us something of what it meant to God to give His Son to die on behalf of sinful man. This scene also reminds us of what it meant to Jesus to take our place in judgment and die in our stead.

In Abraham's case, God, as F. W. Grant has well said, "spared that father's heart a pang which He would not spare His own." So Abraham offered up his son in figure only, and in figure received him again from the dead. We need not dwell on the shock that must have been his when the command first came to take his son and offer him as a burnt-offering. Abraham probably wondered if he obeyed God, how God's words could ever be fulfilled: "In Isaac shall thy seed be called." But faith triumphed over an apparently insurmountable difficulty so far as nature was concerned. Abraham bound his son upon the altar and actually took the knife to slay him, "Accounting that God was able to raise him up, even from the dead." It was faith at its highest, triumphing over every question that the human mind could raise. Abraham's faith depended on the living God, who is the God of resurrection, to work out His own wondrous purpose of grace. Such faith could not fail of reward.

The next character mentioned is Isaac himself, and singularly enough his quiet uneventful life is passed over. It is in connection with the blessing pronounced upon Jacob and Esau concerning things to come that his faith shines out (20). Yet if we read the Old Testament record it would seem as though he had failed completely at that very point, and had only conferred upon Jacob the blessing of Abraham because his wife and younger son conspired together to deceive him (Genesis 27). But the blessing once given, Isaac seems to have risen above his own feelings and preferences, and recognized that God had overruled. Later he confirmed the blessing to Jacob while giving to Esau a lesser one, and in both he revealed his faith in the Abrahamic covenant. We might have thought that faith was at a very low ebb indeed in this instance. But beneath all Isaac's own confused predilections, God made it evident that He discerned real faith in the manner in which Isaac blessed his sons.

In Jacob's case too, it was when he was dying that faith shone out most triumphantly. After a checkered life of mingled self-will and subjection to God, during all of which he was under the divine discipline because of failure, he saw with clear unhindered vision the future of his people. As he was about to leave this world, he blessed Ephraim and Manasseh, putting the younger before the first-born in a manner that gave evidence of the reality of his faith, as he worshiped, bowing upon the top of his staff (Hebrews 11:21). Jacob's life had been a long life for self and a short life for God, but he passed from this world as a worshiper, triumphing by faith.

It may seem strange, when we think of the wonderful life of Joseph, a man in whom faith was markedly manifested throughout, that once more our attention is focused on something that took place just before he died. But in his case his death was clearly the culmination of his entire pilgrimage. Though he attained to great honor in Egypt, he ever realized that his home was not there, and he maintained his pilgrim character to the very last. Therefore, as he was about to die, he reminded the children of Israel that Canaan was their proper inheritance. He requested that when they leave Egypt to return to the land God had given to their fathers, they should carry his bones with them. This might seem a little thing, but God has drawn particular attention to it in several scriptures. It is in Genesis 50:25 that we have the commandment referred to. Then in Exodus 13:19 we are told how this commandment was obeyed when the hosts of Israel went out of Egypt. All through their wilderness wanderings they carried the bones of Joseph, typical surely for us of our present responsibility ever to "[bear] about in the body the dying of the Lord Jesus, that the life also of Jesus might be made manifest in our body" (2 Corinthians 4:10). Then in Joshua 24:32 we are told how the bones of Joseph were buried at last in the parcel of ground that Jacob bought from the sons of Hamor, the father of Shechem. There Joseph's bones rest until the morning of the first resurrection. Joseph's faith evidently looked expectantly toward this resurrection. This hope enabled him to maintain his alienage in Egypt, a type of this present evil world. And so this series ends, and in the next verse another begins.

Varied Experiences of Faith (11:23-40)

Moses, the law-giver, occupies the largest place in this section of Hebrews. In him we see faith working under varied circumstances. Although providence had placed Moses in Pharaoh's house and probably made him heir to the throne, his faith took him out of the palace and sent him into the wilderness. For when he had come to full

age, after forty years learning the wisdom of the Egyptians, he refused to be called the son of Pharaoh's daughter. Recognizing his
relationship with the nation of slaves, he fled from the Egyptians,
and sought a home in the desert. From the people of Israel the Messiah was to come, and because of his faith in Him, Moses "[chose]
rather to suffer affliction with the people of God than to enjoy the
pleasures of sin for a season." For him to go on in Pharaoh's court
acquiescing to the plans against Israel, would indeed have been to
purchase present ease and comfort at the expense of future judgment. He saw that such a course was sinful in itself and its pleasures
lasting only for a season. The reproach of Christ meant more to him
than Egypt's riches and honors, for he looked ahead to the coming
day of reward. If it be asked in what sense he could be said to know
anything of "the reproach of Christ," the answer of course is that
Christ is simply the Greek word that represents the Hebrew *Messiah*. And so for Messiah's sake Moses forsook Egypt. By faith he
gave up all his privileges there and, in spite of great trials "endured,
as seeing him who is invisible" (27). Only faith discerns the invisible God who transcends all circumstances. In the obedience of faith
Moses observed the Passover according to the commandment of
the Lord. He and all Israel found shelter from the judgment of the
last great plague beneath the sprinkled blood. What a picture of that
wondrous place of refuge, which the believer now has as sheltered
by the blood of Christ.

     And as by faith they were redeemed by blood, so by the same
faith in active exercise, they were redeemed by power as they went
forward at God's command, passing through the Red Sea on dry
land. The Egyptians attempted in vain to do the same but were over-
thrown beneath the mighty waters. Hebrews 11:29 brings out very
clearly the difference between faith and presumption. Moses and
his people passed through the Red Sea by faith because they acted
in obedience to the word of God. The Egyptians had no such testimony, but they presumed that they could do what Israel had done
and learned too late their mistake.

     Joshua, the new leader, led the people into the promised land.
Their first victory—the fall of the walls of Jericho after being
surrounded by the Israelite army for seven days—was another

demonstration of the power of faith. But the very catastrophe that brought judgment on the people of Jericho proved to be the means of the salvation of the harlot Rahab. Her faith triumphed over the most adverse circumstances, and gave her an interest in the God of Israel, and a place among His people. She was even brought into the ancestral line of our Lord Jesus Christ.

There were other Old Testament heroes, too numerous to mention, who exemplified the same mighty power of faith. Gideon, Barak, Samson, Jephthah, David, and Samuel are indicated by name (32). It is a comfort to our hearts to see some of these in this list, for we might have questioned the existence of real faith in such men as Samson, Jephthah, and even Barak if we did not have this divine attestation to the reality of their link with God. The goodly company of the prophets, too, are on this honor roll. It moves our hearts deeply to read in verses 33-38, of what this world accorded those whom God delights to honor. Through faith they subdued the foes of God and man, worked righteousness in a world of sin, and obtained divine promises because they claimed them in faith. Some, like Daniel and Samson, stopped the mouths of lions; others, like the three Hebrew children, quenched the violence of fire; still others, like Jehoshaphat, escaped the edge of the sword. Many others were made strong in their weakness, thus evidencing the fact that divine strength is perfected in human weakness. Men naturally cowardly or fainthearted became valiant warriors, turning to flight the armies of the stronger opponents of the people of God. On more than one occasion they received their dead children raised to life again. Others who seemed defeated here were yet to triumph after all. They endured cruel torture for the sake of the truth rather than accept deliverance through compromise, knowing assuredly that they would be rewarded in the first resurrection. Others, we are told, were severely tested by mockings and scourgings, bonds and imprisonment. Some were stoned, others sawed in two, as tradition says was the fate of Isaiah. They were tempted in every conceivable manner; some were slain with a sword, or banished from their loved ones, obliged to wander about clothed only in sheepskins and goatskins, being destitute, afflicted, tormented, finding insecure dwellings in deserts, mountains, and caves of the earth. But concerning them all,

God Himself has written the precious epitaph, "Of whom the world was not worthy."

All of these were enabled to triumph by faith, which as we have seen, is the conviction of things hoped for. They looked on to the future, not receiving in their own day the promise that God had assured them would yet be theirs. He, having foreseen in His divine counsels that the better things of the new dispensation would not come in until our day, left them to wait until after the death of Christ to come into fullness of blessing, "that they without us should not be made perfect" (40).

This last expression is most suggestive and in itself is clear evidence of the conscious existence of believers between death and resurrection. How could these Old Testament saints now be made perfect when they passed away without receiving the promise, if they were not conscious in the disembodied state? It is anticipating a little to draw attention to Hebrews 12:23, but there we find the Holy Spirit insisting on this very truth. We as Christians have now come into unison with "the spirits of just men made perfect." Old Testament saints could not be made perfect in their conscience until the finished work of Christ had settled the sin question. The moment that the veil was torn, the same blessedness came to them that now belongs to all who believe the testimony that God has given. They are all perfected forever in His sight.

In other words, we may say of Old Testament saints that their souls were safe in God's keeping. Their eternal salvation was absolutely assured; but the work on which all this rested had not yet taken place. They were, if we may so speak, saved on credit. In the cross their responsibility was discharged, and now they with us are made perfect.

CHAPTER TWELVE
LIFE IN THE NEW DISPENSATION

(PART ONE)

T he last division of the Epistle of Hebrews deals with the practical outcome that should result from the apprehension of the truth revealed in the previous chapters. We note that this seems to be the pattern in almost all of the apostolic letters. For the Hebrews who had confessed the name of the Lord, their confession had a special application. They were called to move outside the camp of Judaism, with which they had been identified all too long after acknowledging the messiahship and saviorhood of the Lord Jesus. Judgment was soon to fall upon Jerusalem and those who were linked with the temple service. The time had come to separate completely from a system that God no longer recognized because His own Son had been rejected and crucified. All that had been divinely appointed to typify the person and work of Christ was now but empty form. To attempt to reform that system or to restore it to a place in the divine favor was vain. The only path for those who would be faithful to God was that of separation from it all, but separation to the rejected One.

Encouragement to Persevere (12:1-13)

The apostle begins this section with the familiar "Let us" of grace, so different from the "Thou shalt" of law. In considering verses 1-2, the question arises at once as to just what the Spirit of God means us to understand by the opening exhortation. There can scarcely be any question that the "great cloud of witnesses" refers to the heroes of faith already listed for us in chapter 11, and with whom are included all who in every age have walked in the same path of dependence on God. Are we to think of all these as spectators in an amphitheater looking down on those who were contestants in the arena below? It seems to me it is not so easy to decide this question as some have thought. Our English word *witness* can be used in two very distinct senses. It may mean to behold, or on the other hand simply to bear testimony. It would seem as though the original word here used has distinctly the latter sense, so that those of whom we have read in chapter 11 are really testimony-bearers to the power of faith. On the other hand, the apostle clearly seemed to indicate that there is a sense in which we are surrounded by a great cloud of spectators who apparently are looking down upon us, while themselves witnessing to the grandeur of a life of faith. But in any case, it is intended to be a message of encouragement to those who are still in the place of testing.

Believers are exhorted to lay aside every weight and thus outdistance besetting sin. It is not some one particular sin, I take it, but sin that seeks to entangle each believer. No doubt the sin of unbelief is referred to particularly, but unbelief results in many forms of failure. There is no saint so holy but that he realizes he has certain tendencies, which if allowed to control him, would lead to the breakdown of his testimony. To escape besetting sin we are to lay aside every weight. A weight is not in itself a sin. It is simply a hindrance, something that impedes the racer. If we think of besetting sin as a savage beast, and the man of faith running his appointed race with this beast ever following hard after him, we can see at once the striking picture presented here. We who would out-run sin must not be loaded down with needless weights. Each knows for himself what these hindrances are. It is when they are cast aside that he is able to leave the fierce pursuer behind.

The believer must have an object before him as well, in order to keep up his courage to the end. So he is bidden to look steadfastly at Jesus, who Himself is the leader and completer of faith; not exactly "our faith," as we have it in the King James version, but of faith as such. His was the life of faith in all its perfection. In view of the joy set before Him, the joy of having His own redeemed ones with Him in the glory, He went through the bitter anguish of the cross, despising its shame. Now, in answer to all that, God the Father has seated Him as man at His own right hand on the eternal throne. His victory is ours as we recognize our union with Him.

He then is to be the object before the souls of His people. And so we read, "Consider him that endured such contradiction of sinners against himself, lest ye be wearied and faint in your minds" (3). In the hour of discouragement when one feels inclined to cry with Jacob, "All these things are against me," lift up your eyes, tempted one. Look at Him who knew such grief as you will never know, and yet who sits as Victor now in highest glory. Let Him be your heart's object. Let Him be your soul's delight and, lifted above the cares and griefs of the present moment, you will be enabled to run your appointed race unweariedly and without fainting.

And if at times you are tempted to think that no one else has ever been called to endure such trials as those to which you have been exposed, learn to think soberly in regard to this. The fact of the matter is, many have suffered unspeakable tortures such as you have not known: "Ye have not yet resisted unto blood, striving against sin" (4). Here the apostle is not speaking of Christ, but of those who for Christ's sake loved not their lives so much as to shrink from death, but chose death rather than any compromise with iniquity. To this great and final test clearly no living saint has yet been called.

Then, too, it is so easy to forget what is implied in the exhortation, "My son, despise not thou the chastening of the Lord, nor faint when thou art rebuked of him: For whom the Lord loveth he chasteneth, and scourgeth every son whom he receiveth." This is a quotation from Proverbs 3:11-12, and confirmed in Job 5:17 and Psalm 94:12. It tells us that chastening is for our good.

> Naught can come to us
> But what His love allows.

Every sorrow the children of God are permitted to endure is designed by God for blessing. Chastening is not necessarily punishment. It is rather instruction by discipline. It is a divine method used for our education. Notice that there are three attitudes we may take toward the Lord's chastening. It is possible to despise it. He who does so hardens himself against God and refuses to learn the lessons that the chastening is designed to teach him. "Who hath hardened himself against him, and hath prospered?" (Job 9:4) On the other hand, one may faint under the chastening. There are shrinking timid souls who lose all courage when trouble comes. Like Little-Faith in *The Pilgrim's Progress*, they are constantly cast down by the trials of the way. This too is to miss the intended blessing. But the eleventh verse gives the third alternative, and to that we shall come in due time.

"If ye endure chastening," we are told, "God dealeth with you as with sons; for what son is he whom the father chasteneth not? But if ye be without chastisement, whereof all are partakers, then are ye bastards, and not sons" (Hebrews 12:7-8). God disciplines His own children. He reserves the unjust unto the day of judgment to be punished. And in this way we may see the difference between a backsliding child of God and one who has never truly known the Lord, but has made a profession, and then turned back into the world. The backslider will ever be under the chastening hand of God, if he persists in self-will. The one who merely makes a profession may seem remarkably free from any evidence of the divine disfavor. But by this fact he only proclaims that he was never a regenerated person at all, but simply one who bore the name of son but had no rightful title to it.

As children in earthly families we had fathers to correct us and we gave them reverence. Yet they were far from being infallible. They chastened us according to their own pleasure—that is, either as they thought best at the time, or because our behavior was such as to cause them discomfort. How much more ought we to revere Him who is the Father of spirits, who chastens only for our profit, ever desiring that we might be partakers of His holiness. He is never arbitrary in His dealings with us.

The trials to which we are exposed, in His infinite wisdom, do not for the moment give joy, but are often hard indeed to bear. "Nevertheless afterward" the chastening will yield "the peaceable fruit of righteousness unto them which are exercised thereby" (11). This then is the third attitude we may have toward chastening. If we are trained by it and judge ourselves in the presence of God, we will find rich fruit in our lives, which will be to the praise and glory of God. And so the section concludes with the exhortation of verses 12-13: "Wherefore lift up the hands which hang down, and the feeble knees; And make straight paths for your feet, lest that which is lame be turned out of the way; but let it rather be healed." That is, let each believer walk carefully himself, considering those who are weaker, seeking to be rather an example than a hindrance. He should endeavor to recover any who have been ensnared and turned away from the path of faith.

There is perhaps no other truth regarding practical Christian living that is more beneficial for us than that which these verses have emphasized. We are so likely to refer all our trials and difficulties merely to natural causes, and so fail to learn the lessons that they were designed to teach us by our ever patient God and Father. Or else we are likely to take everything of an adverse character as punishment. Thus we become depressed in spirit because obsessed with the idea that we are constantly beaten with the rod on account of our failures. But neither view is a correct one. The truth lies somewhere in between these two extremes. For the man of faith there should be no second causes. Everything will be taken as from the hand of God. Even when one is called to share the afflictions through which the world in general is passing, the humble believer will recognize God's hand back of it all. But His hand is not necessarily lifted in punishment. It is the mind of God that, as a result of the very circumstances through which His people are called to pass, they will learn their own feebleness and the untrustworthiness of their own hearts. Thus they will be cast wholly upon God, who is our strength as well as our salvation. He delights in manifesting His Fatherly love and care to all who cleave to Him. We may be sure of this. When at last we stand in His presence we shall thank Him for every experience to which we have been subjected here on earth. We shall see how in all of these testing situations He was but making opportunities to display His wisdom and grace. And in order to understand His wisdom, it was necessary that we should learn our own foolishness and the sinfulness of our hearts. When these lessons are learned, what blessed fruit results in lives of purity and righteousness. And we learn by these experiences, as we go through them in fellowship with God, to enter sympathetically into the trials of our brethren. Thereby we become helpers of their faith rather than hindrances and stumbling blocks. No one can harshly judge others, or be unkind or unforgiving, if he has learned his own unreliability and need of constant mercy, while walking the path of trial and testing under the discipline of the Lord.

Warning to Continue in the Lord (12:14-17)

In these four verses an exhortation is combined with a most solemn warning. In verse 14 we read, "Follow peace with all men, and holiness, without which no man shall see the Lord." The second half of this verse is capable of being utterly misconstrued, and has tormented many an earnest soul who was seeking to do the very thing that is commanded in the verse when it is understood correctly. A teaching has been based on this verse that holiness is an experience called by some the second blessing, or the second work of grace. And those who do not obtain this experience, although regenerate, will eventually lose their souls and will never see the Lord. But this teaching is farfetched indeed, and finds no approval whatever in the text itself. In fact, the very opposite is true. We follow that which is always before us. When we attain it we no longer follow it. And so here we are exhorted to follow two things, one manward and the other Godward. First, we are to follow peace with all men. That is, we are to make peace our goal in our dealings with our fellowmen. Clearly we will never attain to this in the full sense. Even our blessed Lord Himself, though He came preaching peace, did not find all men ready to be at peace with Him. And the believer, however earnestly he pursues the ideal, will still find men who refuse to live peaceably. Godward, we are to follow holiness. This is to be the trend of our lives. We are ever to seek to become more and more like Him, the Holy One. Apart from this, no man, whatever his profession, shall see the Lord.

The verses that follow make it clear that if there be in the Christian company any man, who despite his profession, fails of the grace of God in not following peace with men and holiness toward God, he thereby gives evidence that he is still a godless person. That is, he is still in the gall of bitterness and the bond of iniquity. So we are cautioned to take diligent heed lest this should be true of any of us and lest any root of bitterness should spring up through us and thereby many be defiled. The reference is to Deuteronomy 29:18, where God warned Israel of the danger to the whole congregation if any individual, family, or tribe among them fell into idolatry. Such would prove to be "a root that beareth gall and wormwood," bringing disaster upon the entire nation. "One sinner destroyeth much good" (Ecclesiastes 9:18). For as we are told in the New Testament, "Evil communications corrupt good manners" (1 Corinthians 15:33). Such a one was the fornicator of 1 Corinthians 5, and in the Old Testament we have a similar example in Esau who, in spite of all his privileges, was a godless person. He thought more of personal, physical gratification than of future spiritual blessing. The day came when he bitterly repented his folly and sought to persuade his father to reverse his judgment and give him the blessing he had formerly despised. Yet he found no place of repentance in the mind of Isaac, though he wept before him and pleaded so earnestly. It was not that Esau himself could not have repented of his folly, though the special blessing was lost for good. But once the blessing was given to Jacob there could be no change, "for the gifts and calling of God are without repentance" (Romans 11:29). The warning of Hebrews 12:15 is a most solemn one, for there were no doubt many in that day, and there are many still who mingle with the people of God but have never judged the flesh in the light of the cross of Christ. Numbers of them will awaken to a sense of their folly when it is too late to obtain the blessing that once seemed so valueless.

Vivid Contrasts of the Two Dispensations (12:18-24)

In the next section of Hebrews 12 the Spirit of God places in vivid contrast the outstanding features of the two dispensations as connected with the old and new covenants. Two distinct circles are brought before us. In the first one are all those who still have their place on the ground of the Sinaitic covenant, and hence are under the curse, as it is written, "Cursed is every one that continueth not in all things which are written in the book of the law to do them" (Galatians 3:10). In the second circle are found those who by grace have been brought into the blessing of the new covenant through faith in Christ and His finished work.

We read, "For ye are not come unto the mount that might be touched, and that burned with fire, nor unto blackness, and darkness, and tempest, And the sound of a trumpet, and the voice of words; which voice they that heard intreated that the word should not be spoken to them any more" (Hebrews 12:18-19). Could stronger language be used to show that no lasting blessing can come to fallen man through the law? The very circumstances under which that fiery law was given should have impressed the lost sinner with his utter inability to meet the law's requirements. Thus he would be led to cast himself upon the matchless grace of God, which alone can undertake for one whose fallen nature is in opposition to the divine will. But Israel, even though they shrank in terror from the display of divine power, self-confidently declared, "All that the Lord hath said will we do, and be obedient" (Exodus 24:7). Thus they made themselves responsible to keep every commandment in order to enter into blessing. Yet we are told, "For they could not endure that which was commanded, And if so much as a beast touch the mountain, it shall be stoned, or thrust through with a dart: And so terrible was the sight that Moses said, I exceedingly fear and quake" (Hebrews 12:20-21). Even the lower creation, made subject to vanity because of man's sin, would not be permitted to so much as touch the mount. And Moses, who might be considered the very best in all Israel, trembled at the thought of drawing near to God under such circumstances. Therefore what possible hope could there be of any ordinary man standing before Jehovah on the ground of legal righteousness?

But on the basis of the grace of the new covenant all those who believe in the Lord Jesus Christ have come into an altogether different sphere. All believers have entered a marvelous circle of blessing based entirely on the precious shed blood of Him who was made a curse for us that He might deliver us from the curse of the law. Note the various items that are mentioned in verses 22-24.

First, "Ye are come unto mount Sion." This speaks of God's free electing grace. We read in Psalm 78:68, He chose "mount Zion which he loved." When there had been a complete breakdown under the former order, God exalted David, the man after His own heart, to the position of king in Israel. He confirmed the promises to David and to his seed after him, and established his throne on mount Zion, which can never be removed (Psalm 125:1). "Out of Zion, the perfection of beauty, God hath shined" (Psalm 50:2). From that sacred mount blessing goes forth to mankind, and eventually in the day of Jehovah's power, "the Lord also shall roar out of Zion" (Joel 3:16). "The law shall go forth of Zion" when "the Redeemer shall come to Zion"(Micah 4:2; Isaiah 59:20). All God's glorious promises will be fulfilled, when "the Lord... shall reign in mount Zion" (Isaiah 24:23). It will be the center of new covenant blessing in that wondrous day. And for us at the present time, it illustrates pure grace superseding the legal covenant. It is not to mount Sinai then, the mount of law, but to Sion, the mount of grace, we have come.

Second, "Unto the city of the living God, the heavenly Jerusalem." This is not to be confused with the earthly city of the great King, which will yet be the joy of the whole earth. For our portion is not to be in this world even when Christ Himself reigns, but we are to reign with Him from the heavenly Jerusalem above. This, of course, is the new Jerusalem, the dwelling place of the bride, the Lamb's wife of Revelation 19 and 21. It embraces all the heavenly saints, that is, all those who have died in faith throughout the centuries, all who in every dispensation believed God and were therefore quickened by His Spirit. The heavenly Jerusalem is preeminently the home of the church and therefore is designated as the bridal city; but saints of all other dispensations who have passed through death and entered into resurrection life will, as one has expressed it, be upon its "burgess roll." This heavenly Jerusalem will be the throne seat of the entire universe of God.

Third, we have come "to an innumerable company of angels" (Hebrews 12:22). The expression translated "general assembly" undoubtedly refers to this angelic company and not to that which follows, and is better rendered "a full gathering" (23, KJV). We have come, in other words, into blessed association with the entire gathering of elect angels whose delight is to do the will of God, and who are themselves learning that will through His church.

Fourth, we are now made members of the "church of the first-born, which are written in heaven" (23). *Firstborn* here is in the plural in the original. The reference is not to Christ personally, but the entire church is called "the church of the firstborn ones," as distinguished from other saints to be called out and saved in a later day.

Fifth, "To God the Judge of all." There is now no separating veil, no cloud of darkness hiding His face. In the blessed consciousness of justification from all things, we stand unabashed in His holy presence. We know that for us the sin question has been forever settled, and His perfect love has cast out all fear.

Sixth, "To the spirits of just men made perfect." These of course are the conscious spirits of saints of former dispensations. They are not sleeping, as some have imagined, all live unto Him. But until Christ's death and resurrection they could not be spoken of as perfect, inasmuch as redemption had not yet been accomplished. They were saved, we may say, on credit, God having forgiven them on the basis of the work yet to be accomplished by His blessed Son. That work now having been completed, they with us are perfected in the sense that they rejoice in the complete settlement of the sin question.

Seventh, "To Jesus the mediator of the new covenant." This was no fallible mediator such as Moses was, who because of his failure was barred from entering the land of promise. Christ Jesus the eternal Son of God, who became man in order to take upon Himself our sin and blame, has met every claim of that violated law. He now mediates the new covenant of free grace, into the blessing of which we have been brought.

Eighth, and lastly, We have come "to the blood of sprinkling, that speaketh better things than that of Abel." The blood of Abel, the first martyr, cried from the ground for vengeance but,

> Jesus' blood through earth and skies,
> Mercy, free boundless mercy, cries.

He died not merely as a martyr at the hand of guilty man, but He offered Himself as an oblation on the cross for our redemption. In instituting the Lord's supper, the memorial of this redemption, we read, "He took the cup...saying,...This is my blood of the new testament, which is shed for many for the remission of sins" (Matthew 26:27-28). That precious blood speaks of His perfect spotless life poured out as a sacrifice on our behalf. In all the value then of His finished work, even the feeblest believer now stands before God and has come into this wonderful circle of blessing.

> And now we draw near to the throne of grace,
> For His blood and the Priest are there;
> And we joyfully seek God's holy face,
> With our censer of praise and prayer.
>
> The burning mount and the mystic veil,
> With our terrors and guilt, are gone;
> Our conscience has peace that can never fail,
> 'Tis the Lamb on high on the throne.

Warning to Accept the Truth (12:25-29)

Based on the proclamation of new covenant blessing we have the solemn warning with which the chapter closes. We have already noticed that throughout the entire Epistle, whenever a truth has been fully developed, a warning immediately follows concerning the danger of turning away from this revelation from Heaven. So to these Hebrews, who were familiar with the claims of the Lord Jesus but some who might not really have received Him in their hearts, the Spirit says, "See that ye refuse not him that speaketh. For if they escaped not who refused him that spake on earth, much more shall not we escape, if we turn away from him that speaketh from heaven" (25). The greater the privilege, the greater the sin of rejecting the message. If God sternly judged those who refused the revelation given in the old covenant, what will be His indignation with those who refuse His present grace in Christ? At Sinai, His voice shook the earth, but now He speaks of a time when He will shake not the earth only, but also Heaven. He quoted from Haggai 2:6: "For thus saith the Lord of hosts; Yet once, it is a little while, and I will shake the heavens, and the earth, and the sea, and the dry land."

The apostle drew attention to a shaking that was yet in view, which up to that time had not taken place. "And this word, Yet once more, signifieth the removing of those things that are shaken, as of things that are made, that those things which cannot be shaken may remain" (Hebrews 12:27). May we not say that already that shaking has begun, and it will continue until all that man has gloried in will be broken to pieces. Man will learn as Nebuchadnezzar learned that the Most High ruleth in the kingdom of men.

Already believers have entered in spirit into this, "Wherefore we receiving a kingdom which cannot be moved, let us have grace, whereby we may serve God acceptably with reverence and godly fear: For our God is a consuming fire" (28-29). It is not merely, as people often say, that God is a consuming fire to the unsaved; His very nature is in view. Consuming fire is holiness revealed in judgment, and God, who is light and love, must consume everything that is contrary to His holy will. For the believer this will mean eventually absolute conformity to Christ, when the last vestige of the flesh has been destroyed. Meantime we are to walk in grace, seeking to serve in newness of spirit and not in the oldness of the letter.

CHAPTER THIRTEEN
LIFE IN THE NEW DISPENSATION

(PART TWO)

The doctrinal part of the Epistle is now finished and the last chapter gives us, as is usual in Paul's writings, exhortations regarding the behavior of those who have accepted by faith the truth declared in previous chapters.

Sundry Exhortations (13:1-6)

Brotherly love is emphasized. Those who have been drawn to Christ out of a world that rejects Him, should be characterized by love for each other. Sadly, it is often otherwise!

Then there follows an exhortation to show hospitality to strangers. This probably refers to visiting servants of Christ first of all, and then of course others of God's children who might be in need of kindly accomodation as they pass from place to place, particularly those who were fleeing from persecution. Some in the old dispensation who thought they were thus showing courtesy merely to men, found it was their hallowed privilege to serve angelic visitors.

Many were already imprisoned for Christ's sake. The saints were exhorted to remember them and to keep in mind all who were suffering from whatever cause, as though being exposed to similar testings themselves. None knew when his turn might come to endure affliction for the sake of that worthy name.

In contradistinction to the loose and immoral ideas so common in that day, and even in our day unblushingly held by many, marriage was to be recognized as honorable because of a divinely ordained relationship. Marriage is to be preserved in purity, knowing for certain that those who violated the marriage covenant would have to face God regarding their sin.

The Christian too should live a quiet consistent life, not coveting what others might possess. He should be content with what God has given, knowing that in Christ he has been granted more than any worldling ever knew. To have His promise, "I will never leave thee, nor forsake thee," is enough. What more could be desired until called home to be forever with God Himself. Therefore in faith, each believer can confidently exclaim, "The Lord is my helper, and I will not fear what man shall do unto me" (5-6). Someone has well said, "God is a Substitute for everything, but nothing is a substitute for God."

> In that circle of God's favor,
> Circle of the Father's love,
> All is rest, and rest forever,
> All is perfectness above.
>
> Blessed, glorious word "forever"—
> Yea, "forever" is the word.
> Nothing can the ransomed sever;
> Naught divide them from the Lord.

The Call to Separation from Judaism (13:7-21)

If we are correct in believing, in spite of what many have alleged to the contrary, that the apostle Paul was the author of this Epistle, we can well understand how earnestly he would plead for complete separation from the ancient system. The glory of that system had departed since the rejection of God's Son. The dark clouds of judgment were hanging low over the land of Palestine. In a little while the sacred city would be a ruined heap. No more would the smoke of sacrifice ascend from Jewish altars. Moreover, most of the apostolic company had either been called home or were laboring in distant lands. Paul himself was very shortly to be martyred by the executioner's ax. With all these things pressing upon his soul, he urged the Hebrew believers to make a complete break with the system that had rejected the Lord of Glory.

First he called on them to remember those who had been their guides in days gone by, who had instructed them in the Word of God. It is evident from verse 7 that he had in mind those who were no longer with them. They were to remember their leaders of the past and to imitate their faith, considering the results of their manner of life. These men for Christ's sake had suffered and toiled, gladly resigning all thought of worldly preferment that He might be glorified in their lives. The object of their faith was Jesus Christ, who is the same yesterday, today, and unto the ages to come. The unchanging Christ, ever abiding amid changing scenes, is to be the object of His people's hearts. It is important to remember that this does not imply that our Lord acts in the same way in every dispensation, but He Himself abides the same in His Person. If this were constantly kept in mind, Christians would not confuse things that God has plainly distinguished. For instance, it is often said by those who do not think clearly that because the Lord healed all the sick who came to Him when He was here on earth, He will do the same today for all who seek His help, because He is "the same yesterday, and today, and for ever." Strange that they do not go farther, and insist that He will raise the dead and restore to them their loved ones now as He did three times when here on earth. Such confusion of mind would be avoided if the differences in dispensations were clearly understood.

The next warning is against false teaching (9). From a very early day men arose in the Christian companies and particularly in Jewish assemblies, presenting new and perverse teaching. It was necessary to warn the disciples against these heresies. Some of these laid great stress on Mosaic and rabbinical commandments concerning meats and ordinances that were connected with the temple service and had no proper place in the Christian economy. And so Paul wrote, "Be not carried about with [various] and strange doctrines. For it is a good thing that the heart be established with grace; not with meats, which have not profited them that have been occupied therein."

In verses 10-14 we have the direct commandment to come outside the camp of Judaism in holy separation to the Lord Jesus Himself. We have an altar of which they who serve in the tabernacle have no right to eat; that is, our altar and our service are all of a heavenly character. Since Christ has died there is no altar on earth. But the altar that was symbolized by the golden altar abides in Heaven, where Christ makes intercession for us. To talk of any other altar, as is done in Romanism for instance, and some sects of Protestantism, is to deny the truth of the finished work of Christ.

> No blood, no altar now,
> The sacrifice is o'er;
> No flame nor smoke ascends on high,
> The Lamb is slain no more.

In the time when the Old Testament ritual was recognized by God, the bodies of the beasts sacrificed for sin were burned in a clean place outside the camp. Their blood was brought into the sanctuary by the high priest when the sin offering was presented to God. In fulfillment of the type, "Jesus also, that he might sanctify the people with his own blood"—that is, that He might set them apart to God in all the value of His atoning work—"suffered without the gate." He took the outside place there to bear the judgment that our sins deserved. Now we put our trust in Him, the rejected One, as our Savior, and confess Him as our Lord. In faithfulness to the call of God we are to be identified with Him in His rejection, so the apostle exhorts, "Let us go forth ... unto Him" (13).

This admonition would mean even more to these Hebrews than to believers in a later day, who have never been attached as the Jews were to a divinely ordained system that was afterwards disowned by God. The deepest affections of their hearts, until they knew Christ, were twined about that system. But the apostle, speaking as a Jew to those who like himself had admitted the messiahship of Jesus, said, "Let us go forth therefore unto him without the camp, bearing his reproach. For here have we no continuing city, but we seek one to come" (13-14). This was a tremendous challenge to these Hebrew Christians. It meant the breaking of the tenderest of ties, and would necessarily lead to the gravest misunderstandings. But in no other way could they be faithful to the One who had bought them with His blood, yet whom the nation of the Jews had refused. They must imitate their father Abraham, who left country and kindred because he sought a city that had foundations whose builder and maker is God.

I need hardly dwell on the fact that this expression, "Let us go forth therefore unto him without the camp," has been gravely abused and greatly misused by many. They make this command the ground for separation from Christians often as godly as themselves, on the pretense that if they do not see eye to eye with them they themselves constitute the camp. But the apostle is speaking of separation from Judaism, and not, thank God, from Christendom. However far Christianity may have departed in some respects from New Testament truth, it has not yet been disowned by God.

In saying this, I would not for a moment be understood as condoning what is admittedly evil and unholy. But we cannot be too strong in insisting that Hebrews 13:13 is no ground for ecclesiastical pretension of any kind whatsoever. Ruin and failure are everywhere in our churches today. This calls for humble confession and self-judgment, not for pride of position.

Verses 15-16 bring before us in a very precious way the sacrifice that believer-priests are now privileged to offer, for all Christians are now holy and royal priests. As holy priests we are to "offer the sacrifice of praise to God continually, that is, the fruit of our lips giving thanks to his name." God has said, "Whoso offereth praise glorifieth me" (Psalm 50:23). As holy priests, we enter into the sanctuary to present our worship and adoration to Him whom we now know as our God and Father. Then as royal priests we go out to man on God's behalf, and so we have the exhortation, "Do not neglect to do good and to share what you have, for such sacrifices are pleasing to God" (Hebrews 13:16, RSV). Our priesthood has both a Godward and a manward aspect, thus preserving that even balance which is so characteristic of the Word of God.

We have seen, in verse 7, how the writer called on the saints to remember those who in days gone by had the rule over them. In verse 17 he stressed obedience to those who now care for them in holy things. "Obey them that have the rule over you, and submit yourselves: for they watch for your souls, as they that must give account, that they may do it with joy, and not with grief: for that is unprofitable for you." True spiritual authority will be exhibited by real shepherd-care of the people of God, and when the Head of the church gives the pastoral gift, it is for the blessing of all. To flaunt such a gift or to refuse recognition of it is to ignore and despise the Head Himself. On the other hand to confuse the pastoral gift with the so-called clerical order is utterly unscriptural. No amount of training or ecclesiastical recognition can make a man a pastor. It is the Head of the church Himself who gives such a "gift" to His people.

In true Pauline fashion the writer begged for an interest in their prayers. How characteristic this was of Paul! He said, "Pray for us: for we trust we have a good conscience, in all things willing to live honestly. But I beseech you the rather to do this, that I may be restored to you the sooner" (18-19). At the most, he realized that in all probability it would not be very long until he sealed his testimony with his blood. Yet if in answer to prayer he might be restored to service for a little time, he would value this, while being in all things subject to the will of God. Who can tell how much each servant of Christ is indebted to the prayers of God's hidden ones? To bear God's servants up before Him is a wondrous ministry. The full fruit of our intercession will only be realized in that day when every secret thing will be revealed and each one will be rewarded according to his own service. Let none think that it is a little thing to pray. There is no higher ministry, no more important office, than that of the intercessor.

The beautiful benediction of verses 20-21 brings the Epistle proper to a close. How often the words have been uttered through the centuries; how preciously they still come home to every believing heart! "Now the God of peace, that brought again from the dead our Lord Jesus, that great shepherd of the sheep, through the blood of the everlasting covenant, Make you perfect in every good work to do his will, working in you that which is wellpleasing in his sight

through Jesus Christ; to whom be glory for ever and ever. Amen."
How blessed is the title, "The God of peace." It is found elsewhere
in the New Testament and it tells of peace made by the blood of the
cross. Now on the basis of the accomplished work of the cross God
is speaking peace to all who trust His Son. After the Good Shepherd offered Himself in behalf of the sheep and shed His blood for
their redemption, God raised Him from the dead thus sealing the
everlasting covenant. God has made that same Jesus to be both Lord
and Christ. Exalted to the Father's right hand, He is now the Great
Shepherd guiding His chosen flock through the wilderness of this
world. Soon, as the apostle Peter wrote, He will return in glory as
the Chief Shepherd (1 Peter 5:4), to whom all the under-shepherds
must render their account. Meantime, by His Spirit He is working in
those for whom He died on Calvary's cross. By this inward work He
is sanctifying His people to Himself, daily making them more like
their blessed Master. All the glory of their salvation belongs to Him
both now and for eternity. And so the "Amen" closes the doctrinal
and practical parts of the letter.

Concluding Salutations: Paul's Secret Mark (13:22-25)

The concluding salutations need not occupy us long. In verse 22
he pleaded with his readers to receive his admonitions, which will
cut right across all their natural inclinations. But because of the
circumstances in which they were found he was pressed in the spirit
to write these words.

His companion Timothy, who had apparently also been in prison,
was now at liberty. Paul and Timothy hoped to visit the churches in
which these Jewish believers were found, if it should be the will of
the Lord. Then once more he mentioned their guides, those who
had oversight in spiritual things, sending to them a special salutation as well as to all the saints. This recognition of their leaders
would come with good grace indeed from the apostle Paul, for there
had been many who sought to bring about a breach between him
and them. But he himself refused to acknowledge anything of the
kind, and he recognized them in their God-given place as caring for

the souls of the saints. The Italian brethren, in Rome and elsewhere, joined with him in this salutation.

Paul concluded the letter by putting upon it what we have seen to be his own secret mark, "Grace be with you all. Amen."

While specifically set apart by God as the apostle to the Gentiles, Paul never forgot that he himself was a Jew by birth. He knew all that it meant for his people to declare themselves followers of the Lord Jesus Christ. His heart yearned over them, and he was jealous with a holy jealousy lest they should come short of their full blessing by compromising and clinging too long to forms and ceremonies that had now become a mere lifeless system since God's own Son had been crucified. He would have them enjoy in the fullest possible way that grace which was the very center and epitome of his message both to Jew and Gentile.

As we review the history of Christendom we can see today how necessary was this cleavage. The heart of man readily falls in with forms and ceremonies. It is only those who are led of God who worship in Spirit and in truth. On every hand men are turning back to ritualistic forms and liturgical systems, seeking thus to make up for the increasing lack of true spirituality and devotedness to Christ. Unsaved men can "enjoy" a "religious service," but only the regenerate can worship by the Spirit of God.

AUTHOR BIOGRAPHY

HENRY ALLAN IRONSIDE, one of this century's greatest preachers, was born in Toronto, Canada, on October 14, 1876. He lived his life by faith; his needs at crucial moments were met in the most remarkable ways.

Though his classes stopped with grammar school, his fondness for reading and an incredibly retentive memory put learning to use. His scholarship was well recognized in academic circles with Wheaton College awarding an honorary Litt. D. in 1930 and Bob Jones University an honorary D.D. in 1942. Dr. Ironside was also appointed to the boards of numerous Bible institutes, seminaries, and Christian organizations.

"HAI" lived to preach and he did so widely throughout the United States and abroad. E. Schuyler English, in his biography of Ironside, revealed that during 1948, the year HAI was 72, and in spite of failing eyesight, he "gave 569 addresses, besides participating in many other ways." In his eighteen years at Chicago's Moody Memorial Church, his only pastorate, every Sunday but two had at least one profession of faith in Christ.

H. A. Ironside went to be with the Lord on January 15, 1951. Throughout his ministry, he authored expositions on 51 books of the Bible and through the great clarity of his messages led hundreds of thousands, worldwide, to a knowledge of God's Word. His words are as fresh and meaningful today as when first preached.

The official biography of Dr. Ironside, *H. A. Ironside: Ordained of the Lord*, is available from the publisher.

THE WRITTEN MINISTRY OF H. A. IRONSIDE

Expositions

Joshua
Ezra
Nehemiah
Esther
Psalms (1-41 only)
Proverbs
Song of Solomon
Isaiah
Jeremiah
Lamentations
Ezekiel
Daniel
The Minor Prophets
Matthew
Mark
Luke
John

Acts
Romans
1 & 2 Corinthians
Galatians
Ephesians
Philippians
Colossians
1 & 2 Thessalonians
1 & 2 Timothy
Titus
Philemon
Hebrews
James
1 & 2 Peter
1,2, & 3 John
Jude
Revelation

Doctrinal Works

Baptism
Death and Afterward
Eternal Security of the Believer
Holiness: The False and
   the True
The Holy Trinity

Letters to a Roman Catholic
   Priest
The Levitical Offerings
Not Wrath But Rapture
Wrongly Dividing the Word
   of Truth

Historical Works

The Four Hundred Silent Years
A Historical Sketch of the Brethren Movement

Other works by the author are brought back into print from time to time. All of this material is available from your local Christian bookstore or from the publisher.